Chinese Export Art
In the Eighteenth Century

CHINESE EXPORT ART
In the Eighteenth Century

Margaret Jourdain
and R. Soame Jenyns

Spring Books

First published 1950 by Country Life Ltd
Copyright R. Soame Jenyns and Basil Marsden-Smedley
as Executor of the late Miss Margaret Jourdain, 1951
This edition published 1967 by Spring Books
Hamlyn House · The Centre · Feltham · Middlesex

Printed in Great Britain by Fletcher & Son Ltd, Norwich
and bound by Richard Clay (The Chaucer Press) Ltd, Bungay, Suffolk

CONTENTS

ILLUSTRATIONS

INTRODUCTION

ASPECTS of the cultural exchanges between Europe on the one hand and China on the other have been closely studied; and the penetration of Western by Chinese influences is fully documented.[1] The other side of the exchange, the export art of China, and especially the production of goods designed for the European market during the long life of the Manchu dynasty (1644–1912), has attracted less attention. The art of this period is China's silver age, but it is distinguished by ingenuity and great technical skill.

Chinese porcelain, lacquer, silk and small curiosities were imported into Western Europe from the late sixteenth century onwards, but they did not arrive in sufficient bulk to create a demand, or to affect European art until the late years of the seventeenth century. During the course of the eighteenth century, Chinese paintings on glass, and prints, painted paper-hangings and enamels were added to the list of exports; and porcelain, one of the largest and most desirable of Chinese manufactures, was shipped in great bulk and variety. In the second half of the eighteenth century, the fashionable caprice for Chinese decoration increased this taste for Chinese curiosities, and for porcelain 'the most innocent and pretty furniture for a lady's chamber'.[2]

From the early eighteenth century onwards, certain tendencies in Chinese were paralleled in European art, a free play of lines, graceful form, virtuosity in technique and an almost 'sweet' colouring.

The complex and disturbed record of the contacts between Europe and China lie outside the scope of this book. From the first penetration to the coasts of China by the Portuguese in 1514 to the end of the eighteenth century, the nations of Europe 'drew a cordon round China both by land and sea, so that at the end of the period the country bore a resemblance to a walled city in a state of siege'.

The position of the English East India Company, chartered by Queen Elizabeth in 1600, was strengthened by a fresh Charter granted by Cromwell in 1657, and for the next half century the Company's attention was directed towards India. It was not until 1715 that a 'factory' was opened by the Company at Canton, and the

---

[1] See G. F. Hudson, *Europe and China, a historical survey of cultural influences*, 1931. A valuable work in which the early contacts between China and Europe are treated.

[2] Wycherley, *The Plain Dealer* (produced early in 1674), Act II, Scene I.

Chinese trade placed on a stable basis. This town became the principal, and after 1757, the only port for Chinese foreign trade.[1] England's lead in this trade eclipsed all other nations during the eighteenth century; in 1753, out of twenty-seven ships trading at the port, ten were English; and throughout the rest of the eighteenth and nineteenth centuries their trade 'exceeded that of all the other companies together'. The system was long lived. On the one side was the English East India Company (and other companies established by the Dutch,[2] Swedes, French and other European states) and on the other a body of Chinese merchants, known as the Hong, who had the monopoly of foreign trade. The factories were rented by the Hong to the companies for the trading season, but when the fleet of Indiamen sailed, the 'supercargoes' were obliged to remove to Macao (Figs. 5 and 6) until the next trading season.

The space occupied by the factories[3] was on the north bank of the Pearl River, on the south-west side of the city. On this ground stood thirteen factories. The rows of factories on the river front were known as 'hongs'. (Fig. 4).

Nearly all supercargoes also engaged in private trade, or acted as agents for British merchants. Supercargoes, surgeons and other officials were allowed space in the hold on each voyage.

This open commerce with Europe drew to Canton a number of skilled craftsmen, and William Hickey, visiting the town, saw there 'the painters upon glass, the fan-makers, workers in ivory, japanners, jewellers and all the various artificers of Canton'. Adjoining the English factory were 'two rows of native houses, called the new and old China Street (Fig. 2), where foreigners might ramble and purchase trinkets'. The port of Canton became known as a place of odd inhabitants and mysterious opportunities.[4] Of the many East India companies, the English was 'the proudest society of merchants in the universe'. When in 1834, the government decided not to renew the Company's charter, the 'China trade' was estimated as the

---

[1] As early as 1670 the British East India Company began to trade with Amoy, but the factory was closed in 1681 and although re-opened in 1685 trade seems to have been unimportant. Du Halde writing about 1730 says that although many European vessels had frequented Amoy twenty years earlier, at the time of writing all European trade had moved to Canton.

[2] The Dutch East India Company was chartered in 1602 and was forced into bankruptcy in 1798.

[3] Beginning at the west in 1825 they were as follows: The Danish Factory, the Spanish Factory, the French Factory, Chung-qua's Factory; the America Factory, the Pao-shan Factory, the Imperial Factory (used by nations not possessing a separate hong), the Swedish, the Old English, the Chao-Chow, the Dutch, and the Greek Factory. There was also the New England Factory with a long broad terrain in front of it stretching towards the river.

[4] F. Brinkley, *China and Japan*, Vol. X, p. 202.

most important of this country's overseas enterprises. In 1854, the Company's functions were transferred to the government.[1]

Goods imported from the East by the East India Company were usually disposed of by auction. The sales of cargoes brought to London by the Company were held at the Company's headquarters, East India House, in Leadenhall Street. Many independent sales were also advertised in the *London Gazette*, and a number of merchants specialized in Eastern goods and curiosities. Several of these merchants were of Jewish origin or Dutch nationality, but English names are also found amongst the advertisements.[2] Retired officers of the East India Company frequently had a rich collection of Chinese goods in their houses.[3]

The advantages of China as a source of certain commodities were great. Chinese craftsmen were known for their sensitive virtuosity, 'their fingers were remarkable for suppleness and delicacy of touch'.[4] The mind of a Chinese is quick and apprehensive, and his small delicate hands are famed for the execution of neat work.

They imitated models sent from Europe 'with the most exact and servile fidelity'. They could meet the European demand for not only was the population immense, but the means of subsistence (according to a writer in the early nineteenth century) so easy 'that it costs scarcely anything to keep a man, and workmen may be had very cheap'.[5] Centres of the Empire became laboratories for Europe. The population of the Ching tê Chen porcelain centre when d'Entrecolles visited it in 1712 at the height of its activity, was estimated at a million. The Chinese took kindly to the imitation of models that came to them from foreign parts, and made 'expressly for Europeans articles adapted to their taste, and images in china, steatite and painted wood are made so cheaply among them that there might often be economy in getting them fron China'.[6]

[1] Dissatisfaction with the British East India Company owing to its jealousy of rivals had excited publicity and called into existence privateers before its final loss of privileges.

[2] Solomon de Medina supplied William III with Indian goods in 1694 (B.M. MSS. 5751); and the name of Mrs Medina occurs in the expenses of the first Earl of Bristol (supplying him with 'Indian cut Japan screens'), *Diary and expenses of the First Earl of Bristol*, p. 146. John van Colema, 'the Dutchman', sold to Queen Mary in 1694 'a fine Right Japan chest, and six Indian fanns with white cane sticks' (B.M. MSS. 5751). A widely known merchant was Motteaux, who had an 'Indian warehouse' in Leadenhall Street, near the East India Company's headquarters (Letter of Motteaux in the *Spectator*, January 30th, 1712).

[3] 'A house called Valentines now in the possession of Captain Raymond of the East India Company is very finely furnished with India goods, particularly there are the several buildings of a Bramin's house cut in ivory, in which he receives people nearer or further from the entrance according to their quality.' Dr R. Pococke, *Travels in England*, Vol. II, p. 258.

[4] A. Colhoun, *China in Transformation* (1898), p. 254.

[5] Breton de la Martinière, *China, its Costume, Arts, etc.* (trans.), 1813, p. 94.

[6] M. Huc, *The Chinese Empire* (trs. 1855), Vol. II, p. 122.

Porcelain, both useful and decorative, found a 'sellers' market' in Europe in the eighteenth century. The Dutch Company employed draughtsmen in China to supply the Chinese craftsmen with designs and to overlook their work.[1] The types varied during the period. D'Entrecolles, writing in 1712, states that little but blue and white porcelain was shipped to Europe, and Le Comte speaks of the export of white porcelain with 'divers figures of flowers, trees, birds, which they paint in blue'. To judge by letters and memoirs, there was a vogue in the middle years of the century for 'shaking figures', that is, figures with movable heads. Such figures were ranged on brackets, cabinets and chimney-pieces, and shelves. Inventories and letters re-inforce the evidence of large accumulations of porcelain in English houses, and many contained 'a noble array of porcelain and other goods brought from China'.[2] During the classical revival in Europe during the late eighteenth and early nineteenth centuries, there was a changed approach to ceramics; and Chinese porcelain was criticized as 'lacking elegance and form' and as inferior 'to those inimitable models from the Greek and Roman vases brought into modern use by the ingenious Mr Wedgwood'.[3]

Lacquered goods in the form of screens, cabinets and trunks were accepted with admiration in Europe, and the distinction between 'right Japan' (Oriental lacquer) and its European imitation (japanning) is noted in accounts. Though the technique of lacquering was imitated and manufacturers of porcelain set up in Europe during the eighteenth century[4] 'neither in porcelain nor in lacquer did the growth of European production eliminate the imports from China. They had acquired too strong a hold on the market'.

The early history of the great traffic in Chinese silk, 'that trade which drew the threads of its exquisite material as a bond of economic unity across the whole of the old world from the Pacific to the Atlantic',[5] lies outside this work. Though there was a decline in the export of raw silk after the silk moth was smuggled into Europe in the sixteenth century, there was no lack of demand for Chinese wrought silk. Chinese woven silks and embroideries, in demand for their novel design and fine and subtle colour, were exported to Europe in the late seventeenth and eighteenth

---

[1] J. C. A. N. de Vries, *Porselein, Chineesch en Europeisch Porselein* (1923) (quoting evidence from the archives of the Dutch East India Company).

[2] Gladys Scott-Thomson, *The Russells in Bloomsbury*, p. 335.

[3] J. Barrow, *Travels in China* (1804), p. 305.

[4] Böttger, J. F., the German chemist and ceramist, had discovered the secret of hard porcelain by 1708 and in 1710 a Royal patent was issued in pursuance of which a porcelain factory was to be erected at Meissen.

[5] G. F. Hudson, *Europe and China, a historical survey of cultural influences*, 1931.

centuries, and in the second half of the eighteenth century St Aubin notes 'that many embroideries . . . have been made for our dandies' on materials sent out ready cut up. Chinese silks, painted in body colour in floral designs, were also in fashion for dresses, hangings and seat coverings during the second half of the eighteenth century.

Much that was exported from China was not made to European order, and would have equally well have served Chinese use. Certain types of porcelain, such as *'garnitures de cheminée'*, pieces decorated with European subjects and paper-hangings decorated with flowers, flowering shrubs and Chinese scenes were, however, export goods.

In the case of paintings on glass and paper-hangings their brilliant colour and fantasy ensured a wide demand, but the art of China was measured by European standards. The realistic representation of birds and flowers was accepted from the late years of the seventeenth century. The Chinese 'are very successful with birds and flowers, which they picture with the needle or on silk hangings so simply that it would be impossible to draw them better from nature'.[1] But the representation of the human form was considered to be 'a high burlesque' and 'either hideous or ludicrous'.[2] Chinese absence of perspective was also disconcerting. 'False lights, false shadows, false perspective and proportions, gay colours without that gradation of tints, that mutual variety of enlightened and darkened objects which relieve and give force to each other, at the same time that they give ease and repose to the eye; in short every incoherent combination of forms of nature . . . are the essentials of Chinese painting.'[3] In time, however, the painted scenes on paper-hangings and porcelain caught the interest of European amateurs, who became acquainted not only with the atmosphere of Chinese life, but also, through pictorial representation, with Chinese gardens and buildings.

[1] Nieuhoff, *L'ambassade vers l'empereur de la Chine* (French edition, 1665).

[2] E. J. Dukes, *Everyday Life in China*. Francis Hutchison, *Enquiry into our ideas of beauty and virtue*, writes that the various contortions of the human body in Chinese art may give some wild pleasure.

[3] *The World*, March 25th, 1755.

CHAPTER I

LACQUER AND LACQUERED

FURNITURE

THE art of lacquering, which was known in China as early as the Shang-Yin period,[1] originated in the discovery of the protective properties of the sap of the lacquer tree[2] (*Rhus vernicifera*, the *chi shu* of the Chinese), a species of sumach which forms a hard, durable, semi-transparent film when applied to wood or metal. This film can be used to coat the surface of almost any material. In China it has been applied to fabrics, brass, porcelain, basket work, pewter and most commonly of all to wood. Besides being a preservative it provides a smooth lustrous surface which can be coloured and which lends itself to painting and carving. The method of extracting this sap or gum from the lacquer trees and preparing it caught the attention of European travellers who described it in full detail.[3] The gum is easy to procure by incisions made on the bark of the tree, but the process of lacquering is slow as each coat has to dry before the next is applied.[4] One

---

[1] See Soame Jenyns, CHINESE LACQUER, *Transactions of the Oriental Ceramic Society*, Vol. XVII, 1939–40.

[2] The lacquer tree is indigenous to the southern and central provinces of China, and was probably introduced to Japan by way of Korea in the sixth century A.D. It is grown today more especially in Chekiang, Fukien, Anhui, Kuangsi, Hupeh and Szechwan and in the wild state is almost confined to foothills from twelve to fifteen hundred feet, but it probably once enjoyed a much wider habitat and grew in places from which it has long disappeared.

[3] See letter of Buonami (dated 1697) in the *Musaeum Kircherianum* (Romae, 1709), also Père d'Hancaville (1760) in Memoir, SUR LE VERNIS DE LA CHINE, *Académie des Inscriptions et belles lettres*, XV, p. 117. (This contains a description of the lacquer industry of the period.)

[4] The *Liu Tzu Hsin Lun* says: 'When a good workman brushes on lacquer juice if he does it very slowly then it is too hard when it dries. If he does it too quickly then it is not hard enough or smooth. He does it not too slowly and not too quickly.' Thirty-three separate processes are described in the production of a first-class piece of plain black Japanese lacquer, twelve of which are applications of thin coats of lacquer, requiring the object to be placed on a cupboard to harden nineteen times, for periods ranging from twelve hours to three days, while the *Ch'ing Pi T'ang* says that the finest carved lacquer pieces of the Yung Lo period had thirty-six coats.

traveller, Captain William Dampier,[1] thus describes the extraction of the gum and process of lacquering.[2]

'The Lack . . . is a sort of gummy juice which drains out of the bodies and limbs of trees. It is gotten in such quantities by the country people that they daily bring it in great tubs to the markets . . . the labourers at this trade (i.e. lacquering) . . . lay several coats of lack, one on another, so these must all have time to be thoroughly dry before an outer coat can be laid on the former. It grows blackish by itself when exposed to the air, but the colour is heightened by oil and other ingredients. When the outside coat is dry they polish it to bring it to a gloss.'

Crude lacquer is a greyish viscous fluid which, after it has been drained from the tree into wooden dishes, has to be strained through linen and simmered over a fire to remove impurities. It turns black when exposed to the air.

Early travellers agreed in their admiration of the lustre and hardness of lacquer. Ogilby speaks of the lustre of Chinese 'shops, houses, tables, bedsteads and all their household utensils';[3] and Lockyer declares it to be 'of so shining a black[4] that you may see your face in it'.[5] Another traveller describes Chinese interiors and household gear as 'so transparent that you can look nowhere but as in a mirror, each opposite object is reflected'. Its metallic hardness and resistance to stains and acids was also an asset. 'It is so beautiful and lasting' (according to Ogilby) 'that they use few or no table cloths at their meals, for if they spill any grease or other liquor on the table, it is easily rubbed off with a little fair water'.[6]

The lacquered surface was 'beautified with several sorts of figures, such as flowers, men, birds, trees, mountains and palaces'.[7] This ornament was raised, carved, painted or inlaid with shell, ivory, jade or semi-precious stones.

[1] Dampier, *A Collection of Voyages* (ed. Masefield), 1906; preface.

[2] The *Cho Keng Lu* by T'ao Tsung Vi (the original of which is dated 1366) says: 'The making of lacquer is affected by the weather. Winter-made lacquer is dark; spring and autumn medium colour; the fourth and fifth months of summer and the seventh month of autumn produce the most brilliant.' Lacquer must be dried in a damp atmosphere and is at all times adversely affected by a dry climate.

[3] Ogilby, *Translation of an Embassy from the East India Company of the United Provinces to the Grand Tartar Cham*, 1669, p. 243.

[4] Charles Lockyer, *An Account of the Trade in India*, 1711. Du Halde also speaks in admiration of the high polish of lacquer 'which resembles a looking-glass', *Description de la Chine*, 1735, Vol. II, p. 177.

[5] The Chinese have made lacquer in a wide range of colours, including yellow, light brown, chestnut, olive, green, black, aubergine, gold and silver, and various shades of crimson and vermilion. In the eyes of the Japanese aristocracy fine plain black lacquer was always held in high esteem, so that it became popularly known in European circles as 'daimyo lacquer'.

[6] Ogilby, *op. cit.*, p. 243.

[7] Du Halde, *Description de la Chine*, 1735 (translated by Brookes, 1741), Vol. II, p. 309.

Exported Chinese lacquer falls into three groups: in the first, the ornament was raised in low relief; in the second, painted upon the surface; in the third, cut or incised.

Some lacquered goods were exported from China in the early seventeenth century, and imports of 'lackwork' by the merchantmen of the Dutch and English East India Companies began about the middle of the century. In the inventory of Lady Arundel's possessions at Tart Hall[1] taken in 1641, 'Indian' cabinets, chests and tables are listed, but such goods make an infrequent appearance in English inventories until the late years of the century. John Evelyn[2] noted the rare quality of the 'Indian' cabinets brought from Portugal by Catherine of Braganza and also speaks of the house of a neighbour in Kent which was 'a cabinet of elegances, especially Indian'. In 1700, Samuel Pepys's home at Clapham was 'wonderfully well furnished, especially with Indian and Chinese curiosities'.[3]

The East India Company was the channel through which much of the merchandise of China found its way into this country. The first reference to lacquered wares in the Company's extant records is in the Court Minutes of 1683 where lacquered trunks are mentioned as sold. The Company's instructions to the supercargoes give evidence of their interest in the quality of imported wares. In 1690, a letter to their chief of council at Tonking complains that the lacquered ware sent over was 'so slight and nought, and of such low esteem' that it did not defray the cost of its freight. Lacquered boards were required to be 'lacquered on both sides fit for screens or pannels, to be done by the best artists and of the finest Lacker works procurable, or else none at all'.[4]

The extent of the trade about 1700 is shown by the records of sales of the cargoes

---

[1] 'In the little closett in the West side of ye Drawing room: a large cubberd fashioned Indian chest; An Indian chest: a little black Indian Table; an Indian standish. In the Parlour chamber: A large cubberd fashioned Indian cabinett, a lowe Indian table with a little Indian chest.' *A Memorial of all the Rooms at Tart Hall* (1641), printed in the *Burlington Magazine*, November, 1911, and January and March, 1912.

[2] *Diary*, July 30th, 1682. Evelyn in his *Sylva* refers to 'that incomparable secret of the Japan and China varnishes which has hitherto been reserved so choicely among the virtuosi' (the ingredients being spirits of wine and gum lac). According to *The Present State of England* (1683) Evelyn first introduced lacquer varnish into England in 1633, which 'in imitating the gold colour has saved much cost formerly bestowed on the gilding of coaches'. (The date 1633 must be an error as the diarist would have been then thirteen years old.)

[3] Evelyn, *Diary*, July 23rd, 1700.

[4] Company's instructions for the supra cargoes of the ship *Trumball* bound for Amoy in China, October 27th, 1697. (Records of East India Company.) In 1701 in a list of goods to be provided at Canton by the supra cargoes of the *Fleet* frigate, they are required to 'bring none except very good and cheap' (January 28th, 1701, MS records of the East India Company).

of three ships at East India House. According to a *Discourse of Trade and Coyn* (1697)[1] 'nothing was thought so fit . . . for the ornaments of chambers like Indian screens, cabinets, beds and hangings'. By the eighteenth century Fukien was exporting lacquer to Java, India, Russia, Japan and Mecca; and Peking and Soochow, Canton and Foochow had become the respective centres of the carved and painted lacquer industry.[2] Chinese lacquer varied in quality. It was recognized by Europeans that Canton-made lacquer was not so fine, nor so much in demand, as that from the towns of Tonking and Nanking. This inferiority was the result of haste on the part of the craftsmen, and too great conformity with European taste. As Du Halde[3] explains 'a work well japanned ought to be done at leisure, and a whole summer is hardly sufficient to bring it to perfection; it is very uncommon for the Chinese to have any (lacquer) beforehand, or that has lain for some time, for they almost always wait for the arrival of ships before they begin that they may conform to the taste of the Europeans'. In another passage he says: 'There is no reason why lacquer objects made at Canton should not have been as beautiful and as of good workmanship as those made in Japan or Nanking. It is not that the workmen do not use the same lacquer and the same gilding, but that those who undertake the work do it too hurriedly and if they please the eyes of the Europeans they are content with it.'[4]

Patterns of cabinet work began to be sent out to China in the reign of Charles II. Pollexfen states that, about 1670, 'some artisans were sent out to introduce patterns suitable for sale at home'.[5] In a document dating from about 1700 it is recorded that several artificers were sent out by the East India Company with 'great quantities of English patterns to teach the Indians how to manufacture goods to make them vendible in England and the rest of the European markets. After which began the great trade in manufactured goods from the Indies.' In 1700 English joiners as a body complained that 'several merchants and others have procured to be made in

[1] Pollexfen, *A Discourse of Trade, Coyn & Paper Credit*, 1697, p. 99.

[2] The centre of the lacquer industry in China during the Han period seems to have been Szechwan. In T'ang times we are told the best lacquer came from Hsiang Chou. The *Ko Ku Yao Lun* mentions Lu Ling Hsien in Kiangsi as famous for lacquer in the Sung period and the carved lacquer of Chekiang was famous during the Yuan dynasty. Ta Li Fu in Yunnan, Nanking, Peking and Foochow all appear to have been centres of the industry in the fourteenth century.

[3] *Description de la Chine*, 1735 (translated by Brookes, Vol. II, p. 303).

[4] By the reign of Hsüan-tê (1426–36) gifts of Japanese lacquer sent to China always excited admiration. After attempts to copy the pieces had failed, Chinese lacquerers were sent to Japan to learn the trade. China, who had once been the master in the art of lacquering, from now on became the pupil of Japan. The Emperor K'ang-Hsi (1662–1722) attributed the failure to the fact that the damper climate of Japan was more suitable for its manufacture.

[5] Pollexfen, *A Discourse of Trade, Coyn & Paper Credit*, p. 99.

London of late years and sent over to the East Indies patterns and models of all forms of cabinet goods and have yearly returned from thence . . . quantities of cabinet wares, manufactured after the English fashion'. So great was the volume of this export that the Joiners' Company petitioned against it maintaining that their trade was 'in great danger of being utterly ruined'. The demand for Oriental lacquer pieces exceeded the supply, and both Chinese and Japanese pieces were imitated in Holland, France and England. By the reign of William and Mary English imitation of cut lacquer was practised. The design of English incised lacquer cabinets is of a convincingly oriental character, for the design was traced from oriental panels. Stalker and Parker write in the *Treatise on Japanning*[1] that the most successful practitioners 'copy out of the Indian as exactly as may be in respect of draught, nature and likeness'.

The practice of shipping models to China appears to have reached its height in the reigns of Queen Anne and George I.

Apart from lacquered goods there was little Chinese furniture suitable for the European market. Lord Macartney observed during his embassy[2] to China 'a want of useful furniture—no bureaux, commodes, lustres or looking-glasses'. Chinese cabinet-work was not (according to Captain William Dampier's report) acceptable in this country. 'The joyners in this country', he writes, 'may not compare their work with that which the Europeans make; and in laying on the lack upon good or fine joyned work, they frequently spoil the joynts, edges or corners of Drawers of Cabinets.'[3]

The Chinese piece most frequently met with is the rectangular cabinet with brass hinges, locking plates and corner pieces, which was mounted on a carved stand of European workmanship. In the inventory of Ham House,[4] taken in 1679, 'one Indian cabinet with a gilt frame carved' is listed in the Picture Gallery. Large Chinese cupboards ('cupboard fashioned Indian cabinets') are listed among the contents of Tart Hall in 1641.[5] A large number of lacquered chests and trunks were imported, and many of these have been preserved in country houses for their utility as blanket-chests. In spite of the number of tea tables listed in ships' cargoes, few have survived.

[1] 1688.

[2] From 1792 to 1794.

[3] *A Collection of Voyages* (ed. Masefield, 1906, Vol. I).

[4] MS Inventory of Ham House, 1679.

[5] Inventory of Tart Hall, 1641, printed in the *Burlington Magazine*, November, 1911, and January and March, 1912.

Folding screens decorated with incised lacquer were much in demand, and though not originally made for the European market, proved so 'vendible' that they were exported in large numbers during the late seventeenth and early eighteenth centuries. Incised lacquer was known as 'Bantam work'[1] in England in the late seventeenth and eighteenth centuries, and is defined in Ephraim Chambers's *Cyclopaedia* (1753) as 'a kind of Indian painting and carving on wood, resembling Japan work, only more gay'. The designs were cut in intaglio and painted. So far as can be determined this type of lacquer originated in the latter part of the Ming dynasty and was imported into England and France before the end of the seventeenth century.[2] The technique consists in overlaying a base of wood with a composition of fine white clay. An English cabinet-maker who specialized in the repair of incised lacquer wrote that the composition consisted of a preparation of clay, finely ground, and next a coating of fibrous grasses. This was followed by at least one (sometimes two or three) coats of finer clay, which was rubbed down to an even surface. On this surface, lacquer was painted in sufficient coats to ensure a body for rubbing down and polishing. The design is scratched on the lacquer ground and then incised with sharp tools, and the hollowed out portions filled in with colours and some gilding. The design is clear cut and follows the style of contemporary painting, so that its date can be fixed with some certainty. The colours of the design, ranging from white to aubergine, turquoise blue, green, yellow and red, are thrown up by the lustrous ground of black, dark brown or red lacquer. Two six-fold screens[3] of red lacquer show European influence in the deep border, which in each leaf centres in the double-headed eagle of the Empire, and in the European costume of the figures introduced. These screens were given by the Jesuit Fathers to the Archduke Leopold of Austria, when he was elected Emperor in 1700. Screens are seldom dated. At Erthig (Fig. 13) in Denbighshire is a six-fold screen incised and coloured representing a cavalcade on a mountain pass. It was a present from Elihu Yale, an East India

[1] Bantam was the name of a trading station of the Dutch East India Company in Java, where lacquer was collected for export. This station was abandoned in 1817.

[2] This method has been called *Kansetsu* by the Japanese. The *Cho Keng Lu* says: 'Bowls, saucers, plates, etc., should be made of the wood of young pine trees cut very thin and stuck together with a cowskin glue; cover with a thick paste made of sand and lime debris from brick and tiles, and cover again with a cloth of linen or hemp, which in turn must be covered with repeated layers of lacquer juice, beaten up with a white of egg, then grind and rub. Inferior lacquerers add pigs' blood.'

[3] One of this pair of screens was presented to the Duke of Marlborough by the Archduke Charles (son of Leopold I) and passed to the Spencer family through Anne (second daughter of the Duke of Marlborough) who married Charles Spencer, third Earl of Sunderland. The other screen (formerly in the Mulliner Collection) is illustrated and described in *The Decorative Arts in England*, chapter iv, fig. 35.

merchant, in 1682 to Joshua Edisbury of Erthig. One example is inscribed in gold to the effect that it was made in 1781 on a lucky day and presented for public keeping by the family of Pa Hsien Liu. Another, in the Metropolitan Museum, New York, is dated 1690 (Fig. 14), and an illustration of another in the Hearst Collection dated 1720 is reproduced on Plate 24 of the *Ostasiatische Zeitschrift*,[1] where a screen formerly belonging to the art dealer is mentioned as dated 1673.

Panels from screens were made up by cabinet-makers into effective mirror frames, cabinets, table tops and brackets.[2] Miniature screens were found most suited for forming mirror frames.[3] Lacquered surfaces were treated as a veneer and in piecing the sections together, all continuity of design was disregarded.[4] Some rooms were lined with panels from screens. This form of decoration is mentioned by Evelyn in 1682 at the house of a neighbour, in whose hall were 'contrivances of Japan screens instead of wainscot'.[5] In a small room east of the State bedroom at Drayton, the lacquer wall lining is preserved. In some cases a screen or panel was sawn down the middle to make two thicknesses. Among lacquered (exported) furniture following the design of European models were seat furniture, and case furniture such as desk and bookcases and knee-hole dressing and writing tables. In case furniture an inscription in Chinese characters is often found on a small space at the back of a drawer.

Any classification of the Oriental lacquer pieces imported into England during the seventeenth, eighteenth and early nineteenth[6] centuries is difficult. In the English inventories, pieces are referred to indiscriminately as Indian, Chinese and Japanese. The confusion can be accounted for by the fact that the lacquer was rarely shipped

[1] N.F. 11. Heft 6.

[2] In *A Treatise of Japanning and Varnishing* (1688) it is stated: 'Some who have made new Cabinets out of Old Skreens; and from one large old piece, by the help of a joyner make little ones such as stands or tables, but never consider the situation of their figures, so that in these things, so torn and hacked to joint a new fancie, you may observe the finest hodgpodg and medley. . . .'

[3] For frames of convex section, lacquer panels were cut very thin, to allow them to be bent to a curve.

[4] Instances of high-handed treatment of lacquer are a chest and cabinet at Castle Ashby (Figs. 19 and 21). In the chest, portions of the border of a screen are combined. In the cabinet the exterior is a complete composition, but for the inner face of the doors, and drawer fronts sections have been applied at haphazard 'without considering the situation of the figures'.

[5] *Diary*, July 30th, 1682.

[6] The carved red China lacquer known as 'Cinnabar' or 'Peking' lacquer in Europe was never made up into European furniture and most of the boxes, vases and other decorative objects in this technique, although they date from the reign of Ch'ien Lung (1736–95) were not made for export, and did not reach the country until the nineteenth century. Many of the large pieces, such as the red lacquer throne at the Victoria and Albert Museum were loot from the Chinese Palaces at the beginning of the nineteenth century.

direct to Europe from the country of its origin, but found its way to some inter-mediate entrepôt—such as Dutch Batavia, the Coromandel coast of India or the port of Canton—before it reached Europe. The term 'lack work' or 'japanning' is applied equally to all these lacquered objects regardless of whether they come from China or Japan. Some of the lacquer imported into Europe in the seventeenth and eight-eenth century was Japanese, which reached the country through Chinese or Indian ports.[1] Nearly all Japanese lacquer found its way to Europe through Dutch ships for the Dutch, confined to the small island of Deshima in Nagasaki harbour, were masters of the field till the opening up of Japan in 1868. This Japanese export lacquer was inferior to the lacquer reserved by the Japanese for themselves. Nearly all incised and raised lacquer comes from China (chiefly from the North of China and some of it possibly from Korea), while the Japanese export lacquer was con-fined to painted or raised surfaces of gold on a black, or more rarely, red ground. There is evidence that Japanese was preferred to Chinese lacquer, and in directions of the East India Company (1699) it is stated that 'none of the wares are to be sent but what are lacquered in Japan'.[2]

The decoration of furniture with Japanese lacquer panels mounted and contrasted with ormolu was a speciality of several French cabinet-makers of the second half of the eighteenth century,[3] and there are large collections of these pieces in the Royal Collection at Buckingham Palace and Windsor Castle, and in the Jones Col-lection at the Victoria and Albert Museum.[4] In the lacquered furniture at Bucking-ham Palace it is more richly represented than in any other existing collection, whether public or private (Fig. 33). During the Regency many pieces of Japanese lacquer were bought for the Brighton Pavilion; some of these retain their original Japanese hinges and handles, but have been mounted in Europe on ormolu feet.

In distinguishing Chinese export lacquers of the eighteenth century from the Japanese it may be noted that the Japanese pieces are usually of better quality, and have a glossier surface. The design of these Japanese lacquered panels is carried out in gold usually in relief (*taka-makiye*). The decorative *motifs* take the form of pre-

[1] Du Bois, *Vie des Gouverneurs Hollandais aux Indes Orientales* (1763). There exist early examples of Japanese export lacquer such as the Van Diemen Box, in the Victoria and Albert Museum. This was made about 1630 in Japan as a wedding present for the wife of Van Diemen, Governor of the Dutch East Indies. The mixture of Chinese with Japanese *motifs* found on some of the exported lacquer from Japan may be accounted for by the presence at Nagasaki of Chinese lacquer craftsmen who worked for the Dutch.

[2] In these instructions (1699) specifications of the goods to be imported included screens, tables and folding card-tables. MS Records of the East India Company.

[3] Salverte, *Les Ebénistes du XVIII siècle*, under Joseph, Petit, etc.

[4] O. Brackett, *Catalogue of the Jones Collection, Victoria and Albert Museum*, Part I, ed. 1930.

cipitous mountains and rocks, with trees and water; figures are rare, birds and animals more common.[1]

In Chinese furniture for the European market curved elements are usually exaggerated and the mouldings coarser. A black lacquer cabinet on a stand in the Royal Collection[2] shows its Chinese origin in the treatment of the heavily curved and moulded pediment.

Apart from lacquered furniture there was a flow of smaller lacquer articles such as tea caddies and octagonal sweetmeat boxes, card boxes, lacquer frames for paintings on glass and fan boxes. Most of these pieces are lacquer of poor quality, usually painted with gold on a black ground, but sometimes of gold decorated in colours.[3]

---

[1] Besides these panels, smaller and lacquered objects such as caskets, boxes and plates were brought to Europe and bought by George IV for the Royal Collection. Some of these according to a document preserved in the Royal Archives (entitled *Notte des Petits Objets d'Ornament en lacque du Japon remise à sa Majesté*) were purchased in 1820, probably by Benois in Paris. One of them is a wooden dish covered in black lacquer and decorated in gold with the Royal arms of England. H. Clifford Smith, *Buckingham Palace* (1930), p. 244.

[2] H. Clifford Smith, *Buckingham Palace*, Fig. 316.

[3] Canton was their usual source of origin, but many tea caddies must have come over with the tea clippers from Foochow. The majority of these pieces date from the early years of the nineteenth century.

CHAPTER II

PAPER-HANGINGS
PRINTS AND PAINTINGS

PAINTED paper-hangings were a developed export industry in China in the eighteenth century, when it is stated by du Halde that the Chinese were 'very skilful' in papering walls.[1] Sir William Chambers describes the Chinese practice of hanging a large sheet of thick paper in the middle of a wall which was covered with antique Chinese paintings enclosed in panels of different figures, and also mentions a room covered above dado height with white, crimson or gilt paper.[2] The only mention of hangings in the form of pictures making a continuous scheme of decoration occurs in the works of Robert Fortune (who introduced many Chinese shrubs and plants into England). He records in the house of 'a mandarin of Tsee-kee', a 'nicely furnished room according to Chinese ideas: that is, its walls were hung with pictures of flowers, birds, and scenes of Chinese life . . . I observed a series of pictures which told a long tale as distinctly as if it had been written in Roman characters. The actors were all on the boards, and one followed them readily from the commencement of the piece until the fall of the curtain'.[3]

References to the use of Chinese paper-hangings in England date from the reign of William and Mary. An advertisement in the *London Gazette* for 1693[4] records the sale of 'paper hangings of Indian and Japan figures', and in the same year the Blue Paper Warehouse[5] announces their stock of 'divers sorts of New Invented Japan Hangings of various colours and Figures', an indication that imitation of oriental papers was in progress. In the reign of George I the walls of a parlour at

[1] Du Halde, *Description de la Chine*, 1735 (translated by Brookes, 1741), Vol. II, p. 150.

[2] Father Louis Le Comte, after describing the use of painted silk hangings by the Chinese, adds: 'others only whiten the chamber, or glew paper upon it'. *Memoirs & Observations made on a late Journey through the Empire of China* (1697), p. 160.

[3] R. Fortune, *Residence Among the Chinese* (1857, pp. 175–6).

[4] *London Gazette*, March 16th–20th.

[5] *London Gazette*, May 4th–8th.

Wanstead are described by Macky as 'adorned with China paper, the figures of men, women, birds, flowers, the liveliest I ever saw come from that country'.[1]

Chinese wall papers were made in sets, forming series of related scenes or designs, with which a whole room could be papered. Extant examples date in the main from the second half of the eighteenth century. A writer in the *World*,[2] speaking 'of the Chinese papers so much in fashion in our great houses', describes the rooms of a house (which were formerly wainscoted) as 'hung with the richest China and India paper, where all the flowers of fancy were exhausted in a thousand fantastic figures of birds, beasts and fishes which never had existence'. After a long period of fashion, there was some decline of interest in Chinese art and decoration during the Regency, when these paper-hangings were used only in 'Chinese rooms'. A cause which contributed to this decline was the great advance in the quality of wall papers printed in France and England at this time, and the novel attraction of French scenic papers.[3]

There is no more direct contemporary example of the depreciation of Chinese paper-hangings in contrast with European productions than the words of the engraver, John Baptist Jackson, who, in calling attention to hangings of his own design, claimed that these were not printed with 'Lions leaping from Bough to Bough like cats, Houses in the air, clouds and sky upon the ground, nor monsters like the figures in a Chinese paper'.

The decorative schemes of Chinese papers were limited. In the largest and earliest group the design is of flowering shrubs and plants.[4] In an interesting group, the industries or the daily life of China are illustrated; while in a third group some figures are introduced in a setting of landscape, or against a background of flowering shrubs. The papers with figure-subjects were dearer than those decorated with flowering shrubs and plants. According to a letter at Dunster Castle[5] 'India paper representing the several stages of a Chinese manufacture upon a greyish ground . . . and a smaller pattern, but the figures very compleat and intersperst with romantick views' could not be obtained under seven shillings a yard, whereas those 'representing trees, birds and flowers of various colours on a whitish ground' were offered

[1] J. Macky, *A Journey Through England* (4th edition, 1724), Vol. I, p. 2. There is no reference to paper-hangings at Wanstead in the original edition (1714).

[2] *The World*, No. 64.

[3] Raynal, in 1770, writes: '*Depuis qu'on a imaginé de peindre du papier en Angleterre et en France, celui de la Chine est moins recherché.*' *Histoire philosophique et politique des établissements et du commerce des Européens dans les Indes* (ed. 1780), p. 668.

[4] *Papiers des Indes à fleurs et oiseaux*, September and October, 1748. *Livre Journal de Lazare Duvaux*, Vol. II, 2.

[5] Sir H. Maxwell Lyte, *The History of Dunster*, Vol. II, p. 376.

at four shillings a yard. These lively and crowded panoramas of figures 'Chinese processions gorgeous and immovable as the flowers and birds, stuck amid gay pagodas and gilded temples'[1] have been described as 'a bright and unmeaning pageant'. But there is a key to the pageant, considered as a display of the life and industries of that industrious empire. References to this group of papers point to their introduction into England during the late eighteenth century.

A Chinese paper of thirteen rolls, decorated with small figures representing the arts and industries of China, was advertised in France in 1781;[2] and three years later twenty sheets of 'India' paper representing the cultivation of tea was advertised for sale. A set of the industries of China was hung at Brasted, Kent, in a house built in 1784. The industries of China is also the subject of a paper given to the banker Thomas Coutts (1735–1822),[3] head of the house of Coutts & Company, by Lord Macartney on his return from his embassy in China in 1794. In this paper hung on the walls of the board room of Coutts's bank in the Strand,[4] the lower portion is painted with figures, which diminish in scale as they reach the upper portion, which finishes in a range of mountains. In one section the potter is seen at his wheel and also in the drying room, and taking his wares to a kiln. In another section cocoons of the wild silkworm are being gathered from the trees, and other cocoons are ranged in trays. Treatment of silk to kill the pupae is also in progress on a tray heated by a small furnace. There are sections showing the sowing and carrying of rice, and the cultivation and marketing of tea. On the latter series, the gathering, drying and packing of tea-leaves is shown, and finally, the transport of tea by boat, and its marketing in a shop, where a merchant is seen calculating with an abacus, and an inscription records that his shop hall 'has all kinds of famous tea'. There is one scene (which seems to bear no relation to the others) in which horses are stampeding towards a small group of spearmen, and also a garden landscape in which an arch bears the inscription that it is the entrance to another world.

There are other recorded examples[5] of this subject, and one of them (a paper of

[1] Mitford, *Our Village* (1832), Vol. II. (The date of this chapter is supposed to be about sixty or seventy years prior to 1832.)

[2] 1781. *En Vente, . . . tenture de papier de la chine, à petites figures representant les arts et metiers, compose de treize feuilles. Annonces, affiches et avis divers*, 6 mai, 1781. Quoted in Havard, *Dictionnaire de l'Ameublement* (ed. 1890), Vol. IV, p. 64.

[3] Thomas Coutts's daughter Sophia married in 1793 Sir Francis Burdett of Ramsbury, and the paper hanging in the Chinese rooms at Ramsbury is believed to have been Lord Macartney's gift.

[4] The room in Coutts's Bank in which this paper hangs measures about 20 ft. by 30 ft., and the height (above the dado) 12 ft. Some portion of the upper part is missing, cut off when this paper was removed from Coutts's earlier premises in the Strand.

[5] See *Country Life*, October 9th, 1920, describing a paper formerly at Beaudesert.

forty sheets imported after 1770 into America) is said to have been brought from Canton.[1]

In three panels of paper formerly at Shernfold Park,[2] the subject is tea-making in a landscape set with pagodas, rock-gardens, tea-houses and water in the lower section, and the upper portion is painted with flowering shrubs, birds and butterflies, on a green ground.

In the series, the pleasures of China, the subject is the lighter side of Chinese life. A portion of a paper in the Victoria and Albert Museum[3] (consisting of two lengths) shows a crowded panorama of festivals and amusements; and in the catalogue of the wall papers in this collection, it is noted that 'unfortunately there is no record of what scenes composed the rest of the paper'.[4] Further scenes appears in a large set (Fig. 44) in which crowds are watching a conjurer and acrobats, and a festival of lanterns.[5] In the complete set and in the fragment, an open-air theatre is seen, with a play in progress on the small stage. One of the actors, who wears a grotesque mask and red hair, represents a foreigner. To the right of the stage is a stand for female spectators. On each side of the stage hang panels inscribed with these sentences: 'the beauty of fur and feathers'; 'all Chinese like it'; and 'to hear the sound of playing and singing is enjoyed even by the sages'. On the foreground, to the right, is a stall with salesmen and customers, and to the left a group of gamblers. In another panel is a procession carrying banners, one inscribed 'when the officials are pure the people are happy', and another 'a short cut to approach your excellent territory'.

In these scenes from Chinese life the upper portion finishes in a range of serrated mountain peaks, and the landscape below is threaded with water courses. In this, the designs of paper-hangings follow the convention of Chinese landscape painting, in which mountains, rocks and water-courses are heaped together in one romantic composition.

In another group of papers, mountain scenery or tall flowering trees and shrubs serve as a background for hunting scenes. In a portion of a paper in the Victoria and Albert Museum, Chinese armed with spears are represented on a rocky island, but

[1] This paper was imported into America by the Philadelphian banker, Robert Morris; the box containing it lay unopened for many years at Marblehead. A large portion now hangs in Mr E. Bruce Merriman's house in Providence, R. I.

[2] Victoria and Albert Museum, E.2847, 2849–1923.

[3] E.3017–1921.

[4] Victoria and Albert Museum, *Catalogue of Wall Papers* (1929), p. 70.

[5] A feast at the end of the New Year, when large paper dragons are carried about, and when lanterns of many shapes and sizes are brought out in the evening.

their quarry is not visible.[1] In the two remaining panels of this paper are boating and festival scenes. A large set of panels showing hunting scenes hangs in a room at Lockleys in Hertfordshire.[2] In this set, huntsmen on foot and on horseback chase deer with arrows and lances; and two monkeys seated on a rock clasp each other with apprehension (Fig. 38). In another panel the foreground is painted with dogs of Pekingese type. From the rocky base of this paper rise bamboos and flowering trees, and the birds flying in the interspaces of their branches add a note of colour. Figures on a larger scale are shown on two portions of a wall paper from the Old Brewery House, Watford,[3] where, beneath a row of flowering trees and shrubs springing from a rocky base, two Chinese are carrying a deer slung on a pole in one panel; in the other, their quarry is a deer and a large bird (Fig. 41).

In a large group of wall papers, the decoration is entirely of interlacing slender flowering trees, shrubs and bamboos rising from a strip of ground. Among the foliage and in the interspaces are brilliantly coloured birds, either perched on the branches or in flight between them. References to this type of paper in England date from the reign of George I. In 1748 Mrs Delany describes a room at Cornbury as 'hung with the finest Indian paper of flowers and all sorts of birds', and later descriptions of this 'bird and tree' design are frequently met with. Their clear bright colours and the realistic treatment of birds and vegetation ensured their vogue. During the 'aesthetic' period of decoration in England, their colouring was decried, and a room at Ashley Park, hung with a Chinese paper, is described in 1882 as painted 'in harsh colours, as people then loved to bear about on their backs and heads in sacque and powder'.[4] The realism in rendering plant forms was noted by the botanist Sir Joseph Banks, in his *Journal*. 'Some of the plants which are common to China and Java, as bamboo, are better figured there than by the best botanical authors that I have seen.' A traveller in China in the early years of the nineteenth century relates this realism to an insistent European demand.[5]

The art of printing had been known for many centuries in China, but little attempt was made to use it for printing the design of paper-hangings, although in the *Handmaid of the Arts*, the competence of the Chinese in wood engraving is recognized, and it is stated that they 'produce very fine outline sketches, which greatly

[1] E.1181, 1183-1921.

[2] *Country Life* (1920), Vol. XLVIII, p. 54.

[3] Victoria and Albert Museum, E.252, 253-1924.

[4] Mrs Haweis, *Beautiful Houses* (1882), p. 81.

[5] 'The Chinese having found that the representations of natural objects are in more request among foreigners, they pay a strict attention to the subject that may be required.' J. Barrow, *Travels in China* (1804), p. 327.

assist in the painting even of very large pieces by means of wooden prints'. An instance of an engraved basis for the design is a portion of a paper-hanging (Fig. 40) on which the design is printed from wood blocks and coloured in tempera.[1]

There is little variation in the design of these papers. In 1772 Lady Mary Coke describes an 'Indian' paper with white birds and flowers on a blue ground as a rarity and a novelty.[2] It has been noted that certain 'tiresome minor adjuncts' such as caged birds, porcelain tubs, and garden palisades appear in examples dating from the early nineteenth century. In some examples, trees and other vegetation are in white, or in colours paler than the ground, as in the paper-hanging, which is said to date from 1811, in the Blue Drawing Room at Temple Newsam.

Chinese papers were packed in rolls in boxes; and several have been found unused and forgotten in an attic or lumber room. The papers were usually backed with a lining paper of linen or canvas[3] and when hung, stretched upon battens. Additional ornaments were sometimes supplied to fill in the pattern and to hide awkward junctions.[4] The design was carried around a room without a break, except for the openings such as doors, windows and chimney pieces. The pattern was skilfully adapted to fit recesses and corners. The paint was similar to tempera but the medium was probably the juice of a plant and not the yolk of an egg.[5]

Chinese pictures and prints of a small size were also exported, to be framed, or to be pasted in groups on walls.[6] An early instance of this use of 'Japan pictures'[7] occurs in a letter to Thomas Coke, dated 1695, and a bill at Erthig includes 'an Indian picture chimney piece'.[8] At Longford a visitor in 1754 describes the chimney boards throughout the house as made of Chinese pictures, showing 'several of their

[1] Victoria and Albert Museum E.412, 413-1914. The two portions (adjacent panels from a continuous scene) were on a screen, the back of which was covered with an English flock paper, with a large floral design dating from the middle of the eighteenth century.

[2] 'There are but eight sets come to England.' *Letters and Journals of Lady Mary Coke* (1889), Vol. IV, p. 137.

[3] December 15th, 1769, Account of Thomas Chippendale and Haig (1769) for 'paper, paste and hanging the room with your India paper upon canvas'. Nostell accounts, quoted in O. Brackett, *Thomas Chippendale*, p. 115.

[4] October 23rd, 1760. (For the Countess of Yarmouth's apartments.) A room to be hung with an Indian paper (Canton pattern) on canvas with some additional ornaments to fill in the pattern; *Great Wardrobe Accounts*, Public Record Office.

[5] Sugden and Edmondson, *History of Wallpaper*, p. 102.

[6] 'Paper pictures to the value of two or three hundred pounds,' to be provided at Canton, are listed in an abstract of goods for the *Fleet* frigate (China Letter Book, 1699–1702, East India Company).

[7] September 22nd, 1698. Letter of Edward Gouge to Thomas Coke asking 'how must the Japan pictures be disposed of?' *Hist. MSS. Comm. MSS of Earl Cowper.*

[8] A. Cust, *Chronicles of Erthig on the Dyke.*

customs'.[1] In some houses, these pictures were assembled to form a Chinese scheme of decoration without intervening framing or borders. In 1742 Lady Cardigan bought eighty-eight 'Indian pictures' and employed Benjamin Goodison (a cabinet-maker whose name appears frequently in accounts of George II's reign) to 'paste them all over the walls of a dining room', and also to 'make good the Figures over the joyning of the pictures'.[2] This decorative treatment was in the height of fashion during the early part of George III's reign.[3] The trade card of Robert Stark (who was in business in 1764) announces that he has in stock 'a great variety of India pictures', and the well-known firm of paper-hangers, Bromwich and Legh, also state on their trade card that they fit up rooms with 'Indian Pictures or prints'.[4] A little later 'a most curious India paper, as birds flowers et cetera put up as different pictures, in frames of the same with festoons, India brackets, figures etc.'[5] was admired by Mrs Lybbe Powys at Fawley Court. Surviving instances of this decoration are a room at Saltram, where Chinese prints are pasted on the walls, the edges being covered by a narrow key pattern border paper,[6] and also the Chinese room at Clifton Hall, Nottinghamshire (Fig. 46), where the Chinese pictures applied to walls are framed in gilt borders. Prints and sheets of Chinese paper were also used in the panels of screens.[7] It is difficult to put an exact date or place of origin to the 'rice paper paintings' (Fig. 51). But it is unlikely that they came into existence before the closing years of the eighteenth century, and almost certainly their original home was Canton. Somewhat similar paintings on ordinary paper go back to the middle years of the eighteenth century. This so-called 'rice paper' is in fact made from the pith of a tree not unlike the sycamore, whose velvet surface was likely to appeal to the decorators of Cantonese enamel and porcelain. The earliest of these paintings seem to have been confined to birds, flowers and insects. It is unlikely that figure subjects (among which are a gruesome series of tortures) appeared before 1800. These pictures are never signed as they are the work of artisans. But the fly-

---

[1] Richard Pococke, *Travels through England* (published 1888–1889).

[2] MS account book of the 4th Earl of Cardigan.

[3] The captain of the *London* in 1772 took back as part of his private trade eight cases of paper prints, painted glass and images.

[4] Trade card in the Franks Collection, British Museum.

[5] *Passages from the Diaries of Mrs Lybbe Powys*, p. 147.

[6] Prints of the same subject are used more than once in the room. *Country Life*, May 24th, 1924.

[7] 1753. 'One will find in the shop of Sieur Prudhomme, dealer in paper, Rue des Lombards . . . an assortment of Chinese paper of different sizes, for wall hangings, over-doors, fire-screens and paravants.' *Mercure de France*, June 1753.

leaves of albums often bear such stamps as 'Yunqua, dealer in pictures and charts, etc.'.[1]

It was not until the Ming period that the coloured Chinese woodcut makes its appearance. During the sixteenth century this medium was used widely for ornamental stationery.[2] By the end of the seventeenth century the technique was fully developed[3] and up to five colour blocks were in use.

The Chinese colour prints sometimes exported to Europe in the eighteenth century usually come from such illustrated books as *The Album of Calligraphy and Painting from the Studio of the Ten Bamboos* by Hu Chêng-yin and the *Manual of the Mustard Seed Garden* by Shen Hsin-Yin. The blocks of the former were cut by Hu himself[4] who was a native of Anhui, a province noted for the skill of its woodcutters, and by his friends. The first edition appeared soon after 1627 and a new edition in 1643. The woodcuts were taken from contemporary paintings and the pictures of flowers, birds and fruit were calculated to appeal to the European and rendered them very suitable for export.

The second work, a manual of instruction in the elements of painting, also contains many pictures of birds and flowers. The second volume of the work deals in four parts with the painting of orchids, bamboo and plum blossom and chrysanthemums, and the final volume with other plants, insects and birds. The first volume appeared in 1679, the second and third in 1700 and the fourth volume not until 1818. As in Japan these coloured woodcuts had a mainly popular appeal and were little valued by the *literati*. The Chinese passed off on the European clients goods which they could supply at the least cost. They did not offer paintings for which there was any demand in their own country.

[1] The only key to their date are dedications such as that on a book of official costumes in the possession of Mr Weinberger inscribed on the fly-leaf 'Jane Buckle, from her affectionate brother Randolph, November 9th, 1839'. The word Canton is often added to similar inscriptions, but such books also emanated from other ports along the coast.

[2] Basil Gray, *Chinese Woodcuts of the Seventeenth Century*. Introduction to C.E.M.A. Exhibition, 1945.

[3] Thus, as Mr Gray remarks, long preceding the Japanese invention of full colour printing which first occurs at the end of 1764 or the beginning of 1765.

[4] He was also an engraver of seals and carved moulds for ink cakes.

CHAPTER III

PAINTINGS ON GLASS

AMONG the few Chinese products affected by the cultural exchanges between Europe and the East were 'Jesuit' china and mirror pictures, both made for export, and both deriving in some degree their decoration from European engravings.

As decorations such Chinese pictures needed no defence. Their vividness of colour added to the gaiety of Western decoration, and the strangeness of their subjects attracted amateurs 'sick of Grecian elegance and symmetry'.[1] As Chinese buildings were dismissed as 'toys in architecture',[2] Chinese paintings were accepted as toys to be admitted to the 'cabinets of the curious', on account of their oddity, prettiness or neatness of workmanship.[3] It was customary, however, to criticize Chinese art by Western standards. According to the Portuguese writer, Semedo[4] (who lived for twenty-two years in China), 'in painting they have more curiosities than perfection. They know not how to make use of oyles or shadowing in this art, and do therefore paint the figures of men without any grace at all; but trees, flowers, birds and such-like things, they paint very much to the life'. A writer in *The World* (1755) speaks of their 'false lights, false shadows, false perspective and proportions, gay colours, . . . in short every incoherent combination of forms in nature, without expression and without meaning' as 'the essentials of Chinese painting'. These pictures were an answer to the demand for paintings, brilliant in colour, that would assort with interiors in the Chinese taste. This branch of Chinese export art was a contribution by the Chinese to the 'Chinese Taste' in Europe. 'This style of painting suits the Chinese artists very well, as it exhibits the splendour of their colour.'[5]

[1] *Letters of Mrs Montagu,* 1749.

[2] Sir William Chambers, *Designs for Chinese Buildings, Furniture, Dress, etc.,* 1757.

[3] Few Chinese paintings, which the Chinese would consider to justify the name, reached Europe at this period. It was the decorations of Chinese artisans, painted for export, which passed in the eighteenth-century Europe for Chinese painting.

[4] Alvarez Semedo, *The History of the Great and Renowned Monarchy of China,* put into English by J. Cook, London, 1655, p. 56.

[5] Douning, *The Fanquis in China.*

These Chinese pictures are painted upon plates of glass; the painting is executed
on the back of the glass, a technique known and fully described by eighteenth-
century writers as 'back-painting'.[1] The manner of painting on glass (in the words
of the *Dictionarium Polygraphicum*, 1735) 'is quite contrary to that of limning or
painting on cloth or wood, for in this, the paint being put on one side is plainly
visible on the other'. Descriptions of the process of painting upon glass are found in
Amiot's *Mémoires concernant l'histoire, les sciences, les arts, les moeurs, les usages* (etc.)
des Chinois, and in de Guigne's *Voyages*. According to de Guigne[2] Chinese artists
preferred clear to mirror glass as a basis for their painting, because the thicker plate
of mirror glass modified the colours. They generally used oil[3] paints and sometimes
colours mixed with a gum. When painting upon mirror glass the artist first traced
the outlines of his design, then removed the amalgam of tin and mercury where
necessary with a special steel tool, to have a clear space for his painting.

In Amiot's *Mémoires* the process of painting on glass and the skill of the Chinese
artist in this technique is described, and the art is stated to have been introduced
from Europe, probably by Jesuit missionaries.[4]

Painting upon glass is mentioned as one of the accomplishments of the Jesuit
missionary Father Castiglione (1688–1766), who came to Pekin in 1715 and passed
most of his life there. He won the favour of two Emperors[5] who entrusted him with
the decorations of the Imperial Garden in Pekin. According to Huc,[6] Castiglione
learned to paint 'patiently' in oil on glass, and in water colours on silk, his subjects
being 'trees, fruit, animals of every species, but rarely figures'. Amiot writes that

[1] Of painting on the reverse side of glass with a background of silver leaf, there are several early
Italian examples, mostly of a religious character, in the Victoria and Albert Museum; of English
back-paintings on glass there are the panels of the Vyvyan Salt (Victoria and Albert Museum),
drawn from Whitney's *Choice of Emblems* (1586), and a few armorial panels.

[2] 'Les Chinois préfèrent le verre ordinaire à la glace parceque les couleurs s'y attachent mieux,
et que d'ailleurs, étant plus mince, la couleur ne change pas autant en traversant l'épaisseur. Ils
peignent sur verre à la gomme et à l'huile. Mais la dernière manière est plus en usage. Lorsqu'il
s'agit de peindre sur une glace étamée, ils commencent par dessiner le contour des objets et enlèvent
en suite avec un outil d'acier fait exprès, le vivargent ou le tain, à la place duquel ils mettent de la
couleur.' C. de Guigne, *Voyages à Peking*, 1784–1801. Paris 1808. Vol. II, pp. 239–40.

[3] Painting in oil is said to have been introduced by a missionary, Father Gherardini (S.J.), who
reached Pekin in 1699. 'The Emperor (K'ang Hsi) being desirous of keeping in touch with European
technique, one of the fathers returned to France to fetch more missionaries with greater specialist
knowledge of science and art. He brought back with him Gherardini, S.J., a painter.' M. Paléologue,
L'Art Chinois (1887).

[4] *Mémoires concernant l'histoire, les sciences, les arts . . .* (etc.) *des Chinois* (Paris, 1786). Vol. II,
p. 363.

[5] Yung Chêng and Ch'ien Lung.

[6] Huc, *Le Christianisme*, Vol. IV, pp. 71–2.

Father Castiglione and Father Attiret were commissioned by the Emperor to paint some large mirrors.[1]

An early reference to a Chinese mirror picture is quoted in Savary des Bruslons' *Dictionnaire universel de commerce*,[2] where a French writer speaks of the difficulty of back-painting and states that it was then (1745) almost unknown in France.

'When I was in Port Louis in 1745 I saw a Chinese mirror which had been sent the Marquis de Roturier, whereon was seen a Chinese lady at her toilet; above her in one corner a parrot on its perch, and behind it a monkey. Overcome by the beauty of the mirror and the skill of the workmanship, I tried eagerly to discover by what means I could imitate it. When, after much careful thought, I believed I had solved the problem, I secured the help of Monsieur Desnoyers, manager of the magazine at the citadel of Port Louis, who was a very skilful painter. Together we worked out my idea and had the happiness to achieve a result which seemed to both of us highly satisfactory.' In nearly every landscape in these pictures, there is a sheet of calm water, a lake or river, either near at hand or in the distance; and this, very thinly painted, does not entirely obscure the reflecting surface of the glass.

European prints were sent out and copied with varying degrees of success. 'A case of prints after Poussin, Mignard' is listed among the goods sent from France in the ship *Amphitrite*, and a writer in 1804 states that the 'coloured prints of Europe that are carried out to Canton are copied there with the most wonderful fidelity'.[3]

But though French and Dutch engravings were imported into China, and many pieces of Chinese porcelain were decorated with subjects copied from the prints, the subjects of few mirror pictures have been identified.

The plates of mirror glass were imported from Europe for decoration by Chinese painters and in 1764 Elie de Beaumont speaks of mirrors sent from England, painted in China and then returned.[4] This importation of glass was necessary, for Breton de la Martinière speaks of Canton as having the only glass house in the Empire. 'Looking glasses and glass mirrors', he writes, 'have been manufactured there, quicksilvered in the European manner, but this undertaking has not proved successful. The manufacturers do not know how to manufacture it with the proper materials.'[5]

[1] *Mémoires*, p. 363.

[2] Savary des Bruslons, *Dictionnaire universel de commerce* (ed. 1761).

[3] J. Barrow, *Travels in China* (1804), p. 327.

[4] *Diary*, 1764, quoted in the *Revue Britannique* (1895), Vol. III.

[5] Breton de la Martinière, *China, its costume, arts, etc.*, translated, 1813, p. 116.

In Chinese pictures on glass of the middle years of the eighteenth century there is a curious amalgam of Chinese and European elements. The subjects, such as groups of well-to-do Chinese men and women 'leading a life of ease and pleasure under shady trees',[1] or Chinese ladies seated in attitudes of aristocratic passivity in a garden or pastoral landscape were designed to attract Western buyers. In two paintings, the subject is reversed (Figs. 57 and 58).

In the last years of the eighteenth and early nineteenth centuries there are references to the copies made in China of European (especially French) originals; and these copies are praised for their merit 'peculiar to themselves, derived from the brilliancy of the colours, and from the ornaments added, in China, particularly those of the vegetable kingdom'.[2] Trees and shrubs are freely introduced, but with no symbolic intention. Towards the end of the eighteenth century exact and imitative copies of European pictures or prints were executed. Writing of paintings of this period Sir George Staunton[3] speaks of the closeness of the copies of European prints, which attracted the notice of a 'gentleman eminent for his taste in London' who had in his possession a coloured copy made in China of a print from a study of Sir Joshua Reynolds, which he deems not unworthy of being added to his collection of valuable paintings. A European source is indicated by some subjects, such as a glass picture (formerly in the Stephen Winkworth collection) in which a girl in transparent draperies stands in front of a figure of Pan.

The painters of these pictures are not known and no signed example has come to light of earlier date than the nineteenth century. To this period belongs a small picture of a girl (Fig. 67) having on the backboard the trade label of 'Falqua painter in oils and water colours and on glass. China Street, Canton'. China Street was one of the streets in Canton where foreigners might ramble and purchase goods.

Canton is mentioned as a centre of painting on glass by de Guigne, and Amiot speaks of painters from Canton employed in painting on mirrors at Pekin. William Hickey when in Canton in 1768 was taken to see the 'most celebrated painters upon glass'.[4] The vast majority of the glass paintings with landscape and water suggest this neighbourhood. For a feature of Canton is the Pearl River, or Chu Kiang, which

[1] Soame Jenyns, *A Background to Chinese Painting*, p. 132.

[2] Moreau de Saint-Méry, *An Authentic Account of the Embassy of the Dutch East India Company to the Emperor of China in the year* 1794–5. Taken from the *Journal* of A. E. van Braam.

[3] Sir G. Staunton, *Embassy to China*, 1798, p. 125. 'The Canton artists are uncommonly expert in imitating European works, they mend and even make watches, copy paintings and colour drawings with great success.' *Ibid.*, Vol. III, p. 385.

[4] *Memoirs of William Hickey* (1769–75), Vol. I, p. 200.

flows through the suburbs of the city for five or six miles and intersects them with numerous creeks and tributaries. In a large number of mirror pictures a broad navigable river appears, with its surface filled with house-boats and all sorts of craft, and its banks set with houses and gardens (Fig. 54). The terrain at Macao is very similar and may be represented in some of these pictures. 'Nothing appears more extraordinary to the eyes of a stranger at Canton than the innumerable boats of different sizes with which the river is covered for many miles together.'

The attractive ornaments added are, to a great extent, of 'the vegetable kingdom'. Among the flowers, trees or shrubs which are frequently represented are the tree peony, the rose, the lotus, the peach and chrysanthemum. Among birds the very decorative golden pheasant is a favourite, but the Manchurian crane, the Mandarin teal and the Burmese peacock are also depicted. Most of the birds and flowers introduced (apart from some stock felicitous emblems) suggest the South of China rather than the North.

The subjects fall into three groups:

1. *Still life paintings* of flowers, flowering shrubs and utensils; and pictures of birds.

2. *Single figures or groups of figures in a Chinese setting or landscape.* In one mirror painting, dating from about 1765, the two women represented, who wear Chinese dress, are of European type. A contemporary inscription on the backboard records that the subject is a view of the river at Canton, China, with portraits of Frances Revell, wife of Henry Revell, China Civil Service (for nineteen years head supercargo to the Honourable East India Company), and her eldest daughter Frances.

3. *Scenes and figure-subjects of Chinese interest.* To this class belongs the pair of pictures from the collection of the late Amyand John Hall (grandson of the original owner, Richard Hall, who resided in China from 1785 to 1803). The tradition of the Hall family is that the pictures were painted for Richard Hall in China soon after he returned to England. Of the two pictures, which are painted on glass of exceptional dimensions, one represents the Emperor (distinguished by the Imperial dragons on his coat) seated on a terrace before a tent with a walled palace in the background. Behind him are men of military rank, and his two consorts. To the right there is a group of archers carrying bows protected by cases; and one kneeling figure in the centre is about to make, or has just made, the *Kow-tow*. The scene is wintry, the mountains and plain are covered with snow (Fig. 66).

In the companion picture an Empress with her ladies are represented in the grounds of a palace laid out with a lake and pavilions (probably the old summer palace which was destroyed in 1860). The Emperor bears some resemblance to Chia Ch'ing (1796–1821) whose reign would coincide with the date given by the Hall family tradition. To this class belongs a mirror picture of three Immortals (in the collection of Mrs Stephen Winkworth) which is inscribed (in Chinese) 'the three stars are here'.

Amiot speaks of pornographic painting on glass after Western originals. '*Les Chinois n'ont que trop bien réussi à peindre sur de grandes et de petites glaces, les saletés et les infamies cyniques dont on leur avait donné des modèles.*'[1]

Perhaps Amiot would include in his condemnation pictures in which women are shown lightly clad, or clad in transparent stuffs, or half hidden by a curtain. For it appears that almost the only use to which the Chinese put these glass paintings in their own country was as a decoration for the interiors of their *maisons tolerés*, and their theatres; so that some of these lightly clad ladies were probably painted for Chinese consumption. The painting was of course the work of artisans and seldom signed and as in the case of the so-called 'rice paper' paintings considered by the Chinese as trivialities beneath any serious notice. No mention of such work appears in any Chinese books on painting.[2]

Glass pictures remained in demand in the early nineteenth century, and a writer in 1838 speaks of English sailors as 'very much caught by this showy material', and carrying away some trumpery specimens to dazzle the eyes of the fair dames of Shadwell and Blackwall.[3]

The frames, of Chinese workmanship, were either of hard wood, or soft wood lacquered (Fig. 60). When framed in this country, the carved and gilded frames of the rococo period added to the effectiveness of pictures painted on glass. Sir William Chambers describes a gallery at Kew House, in which in the piers between the windows were 'four large painted looking glasses from China'.[4] Frames of the

---

[1] *Mémoires concernant l'histoire (etc.) des Chinois* (1786), Vol. II, p. 363.

[2] Small glass vases and snuff-bottles elaborately painted with birds and flowers and sometimes with European subjects and signed *Ku Yüeh Hsüan* (Ancient moon pavilion) (which appears to have been the studio name of artists called Hu, who worked in the Ch'ien Lung period (1736–1796)) are highly prized by the Chinese. In Vol. II, *The Illustrated Catalogue of the Chinese Government's Exhibits for the International Exhibition of Chinese Art in London*, pp. 32–34, 1936, it is stated that this *Ku Yüeh Hsüan* mark was put on pieces made for a private individual and not inscribed on glass vessels made for the imperial palaces, but the compiler is unable to identify the studio from which the mark emanated. Later glass snuff-bottles painted very ingeniously on the inside surface often carry the names of *Ma Shao Hsüan* (*circa* 1880) and *Chi I-chung* (*c.* 1879).

[3] Douning, *The Fanquis in China*, 1838, Vol. 2, p. 112.

[4] *Plans, Elevations [etc.] of the Gardens and Buildings at Kew* (1763).

middle years of the century show the influence of the *Director* period of design. There are frames of carved and gilt wood surrounding two Chinese pictures on glass at Saltram[1] dating from about 1750–1760. At Harewood House, Yorkshire, a frame designed in the classical taste by Robert Adam dates from about 1765. The glass picture it frames is described in 1819 as 'an elegant Indian glass, adorned with their king, queen and attendants'.[2]

[1] *Country Life*, January 30th, 1926, p. 166.
[2] Jewell, *The Tourist's Companion to Harewood*, 1819, p. 24.

CHAPTER IV

PORCELAIN

THE collecting and display of porcelain, which added something to the gaiety of Western decoration, dates in England only from the late seventeenth century, when supplies were shipped to Europe in sufficient quantities to create a demand. In England the collection of porcelain was in fashion in William III's reign; and John Evelyn who visited Kensington Palace in 1696 noted a 'great collection of porcelain'.[1] The 'humour' of china collecting was introduced by Queen Mary, and the inventory of the contents of Kensington Palace (drawn up in 1696) is evidence of the size of her collection. Daniel Defoe speaks of furnishing houses with chinaware as a novelty which had increased so that china was piled 'upon the tops of cabinets, scrutores and every chimneypiece to the tops of the ceilings . . . . till it became a grievance in the expense of it and was injurious to their families and estates'. There is ample evidence of the size of collections and of the ardour of collectors, who ransacked India-houses for porcelain and oriental goods, and searched East Indiamen on their arrival in port.

A number of collections of porcelain in the Chinese cabinets of German palaces have been listed, such as the Chinese apartments in Ludwigsburg, the mirror cabinet in the old Royal Palace in Munich (destroyed by fire in 1729), and Augustus the Strong's collection in Dresden.

Chinese export porcelain made for the European market in the eighteenth century can be divided for convenience into five categories:

(*a*) Pieces which bear no trace of foreign influence, either in shape or design. Most of the exported K'ang Hsi blue and white and *famille verte* (other than the armorial pieces) falls into this class.

(*b*) Pieces made in European shapes, copied from European ceramics, silver or glass.

(*c*) Pieces decorated in China with European designs for the foreign market. (This includes armorial services and the so-called 'Jesuit' china.)

[1] *Diary*, April 23rd, 1696.

(*d*) Pieces exported to Europe in the white, and decorated by European artists. This group is not a branch of Chinese ceramic art, but is included here because the European decoration is sometimes confused with Chinese renderings of European subjects.

(*e*) Pieces (chiefly blue and white) to which decoration was added in Europe. This is covered by the term clobbered wares.

It is impossible to distinguish between many of the wares made in the reign of K'ang Hsi for the home, and those made for the European, market. 'Certain types of painting not specially European in style, and certain forms (such as the set of three vases and two beakers known as *garniture de cheminée*) were found to be popular and continued to be made for foreigners.'[1]

There is a well-known type of export ware consisting of sets of vases with complex moulding, and dishes and plates with petal-shaped lobes on the sides or borders. 'The central design of the decoration commonly consists of *ch'i lin* and phoenix, sea monsters (*hai shou*), storks or ducks beside a flowering tree, or some such familiar pattern, and the surrounding petal-shaped panels are filled each with a growing flower, or a vignette of bird and plant, plant and insect, or even a small landscape. These bright but often perfunctorily painted wares are paralleled in the early K'ang Hsi blue and white. They are among the first Chinese polychrome porcelains to be copied by the European potters.'[2] Quantities[3] of K'ang Hsi blue and white were ordered by the Dutch and other East Indian Companies direct from Ching-tê Chên, and many of these pieces were mounted in silver mounts in Europe. Some, despite the Chinese designs, are European in shape, the porcelain is of the highest class with a crisp white body and oily glaze, and underglaze blue, which are up to the standards of the home market.

It was not until the early years of the eighteenth century that the blue became increasingly grey, the decoration summary and the body coarse. As late as the middle years of the nineteenth century the blue and white 'Nanking China' (as it was commonly called) continued to be shipped in quantities to Europe. A few types which are neither of true Chinese taste nor made to European design are peculiar to this export trade. The so-called Batavian ware, with coffee-brown ground and bold *famille rose* panels, is an early type taking its name from the Dutch trading-

[1] W. B. Honey, *The Ceramic Art of China and Other Countries of the Far East*, p. 157.

[2] R. L. Hobson, *Chinese Pottery and Porcelain*, Vol. II, p. 167. On plate 107 two covered vases and a plate of this type are illustrated.

[3] For example, castors, mustard pots, candlesticks, salt cellars, and by the Yung Chêng period, castors, samovars and even bidets and *bourdalous*.

station in Java. Later in the eighteenth century a class of jars known as 'Mandarin porcelain' became very popular and inspired the patterns used at several English porcelain-factories. In the last phase of the East India Company's trade with China, in the second quarter of the nineteenth century, a barbarous celadon with *famille rose* enamelling was much exported, together with many bowls and plates painted with crowded flowers mainly in green, pink and opaque white on a gilt ground.[1]

The town of Ching-tê Chên has been since the beginning of the Ming dynasty the centre[2] of the ceramic industry of China and at least eighty per cent of the fine porcelain was made there. The Jesuit priest Père d'Entrecolles has left an account of the place in two letters,[3] one in 1712 (at the height of the K'ang Hsi period), and his second in 1722, at its close. These give a description of the town and its kilns, whose whirling flames gave at night 'the appearance of a burning town', and the 'huge population, estimated at a million souls, all directly or indirectly interested in the products of its three thousand kilns'. Here there was work even for the halt and the blind, young and old, women and children, collecting firewood, tending the furnaces and grinding colours.

Le Comte (writing as early as 1699) was vexed by the indiscriminate taste of the foreigner complaining that 'the European merchants no longer deal with good artists, and having no knowledge of these matters take what the Chinese offer them'. The demand for blue and white by foreign merchants was insatiable.[4] D'Entrecolles notes that they bought little else.[5]

These merchants demanded large, bizarre and highly decorated pieces. Many of these pieces were built up in sections from moulds and loaded with strange ex-

---

[1] Honey, *op. cit.*, p. 157.

[2] Hobson describes it as 'A large unwalled town or mart on the south bank of the Ch'ang river in the north-east of the province of Kiangsi. This river flows into the Poyang Lake, which is connected with the Yangtse, so that the wares of Ching-tê Chên can be carried by water to that great highway of commerce, or southward by the Kan river (which also flows into the Poyang Lake) and the North river to Canton. They are also transported by coolies overland into Anhwei and other parts.'

[3] S. Bushell, *Chinese Pottery and Porcelain*, Appendix, where two letters are reproduced in full; or *Lettres édifiantes et curieuses écrites des missions étrangers par quelques missionaires de la Compagnie de Jésus*, Vols. XII and XVI.

[4] Most of this porcelain was ordered direct from Ching-tê Chên in the K'ang H'si period by foreign merchants, the largest quantities by the Dutch.

[5] '*Pour ce qui est des couleurs de la porcelaine, il y en a de toutes les sortes. On n'en voit guères en Europe que de celle qui est d'un bleu vif sur un fond blanc. Je crois pourtant que nos marchands y en ont apporté d'autres.*' Bushell, *op. cit.*, Appendix, p. 193.

crescences. The Chinese had to ask high prices for them, as they had no sale in China, and the European markets rejected them if they were flawed.[1]

The Chinese officials on their part continually pressed D'Entrecolles to supply European designs, which might interest the Chinese Court.[2]

It is probable that a few of the finer pieces, generally classed as export porcelain because of their European shape or decoration, were made for the palace, and it seems unlikely that all the puzzle jugs made in imitation of Dutch Delft, and the grotesque European figures from Fukien, were made exclusively for the foreign market. Most of the jars of enormous size (except the dragon bowls) were for foreign consumption. Four-foot jars were made in 1722 to the order of Canton merchants, who dealt with Europeans; and Augustus the Strong of Saxony is said to have purchased a set of monster vases for the price of a regiment of soldiers.

Pieces of export porcelain made for the European market were often copies of European ceramics, silver and glass, characteristic French faience forms such as flower-pot holders (*cachepots*) and wall cisterns with their basins for export.

A blue and white punch bowl[3] with a scalloped edge is illustrated by Jones, copied from a silver shape (the Monteith) in vogue between 1686–90.[4] A coffee-pot

[1] 'D'ailleurs la porcelaine qu'on transporte en Europe, se fait presque toujours sur des modèles nouveaux, souvent bisarres et où il est difficile de réussir: pour peu qu'elle ait de défaut, elle est rebutée des Européens qui ne veulent rien que d'achevé, et des-là elle demeure entre les mains des ouvriers, qui ne peuvent la vendre aux Chinois parce qu'elle n'est pas de leur goust. . . . J'ay dit que la difficulté qu'il y a d'exécuter certains modèles venus d'Europe, est une des choses qui augmente le prix de la porcelaine: car il ne faut pas croire que les ouvriers puissent travailler sur tous les modèles qui leur viennent des pays étrangers. Il y en a d'impraticables à la Chine, de mêsme qu'il s'y fait des ouvrages qui surprennent les etrangers, et qu'ils ne croyent pas possibles.' Bushell, Appendix, *op. cit.*, pp. 202 and 203.

[2] 'Les Mandarins qui sçavent quel est le génie des Européens en fait d'invention, m'ont quelquefois prié de faire venir d'Europe des desseins nouveaux et curieux, afin de pouvoir presenter à l'Empereur quelque chose de singulier. D'un autre costé les Chrestiens me pressoient fort de ne point fournir de semblables modèles, car les Mandarins ne sont pas tout à fait si faciles à se rendre que nos Marchands, lorsque les ouvriers leur disent qu'un ouvrage est impractiquable, et il y a souvent bien des bastonnades données, avant que le Mandarin abandonne un dessein dont il se promettoit de grands avantages.' Bushell, *op. cit.*, Appendix, p. 204.

[3] Alfred Jones, 'Old Chinese porcelain made from English silver models', *Burlington Magazine*, Vol. XX, October 1911–March 1912.

[4] Jones says: 'It may not therefore be a rash guess to assign the date of this punch bowl to the few years between 1686 and 1690 when the highly popular Monteith bowl was first introduced into England. Allusion has just been made to the rarity of the prototype of this bowl. It will not be out of place to mention four examples: the earliest is of the year 1680–1681 in the possession of the Drapers' Company. The others, forming a pair of the same shape dating from the first years of the short reign of James II, 1685–86, are in the fine collection of the plate of the Skinners' Company and were given by Richard Chiverton. Another example of the same date decorated with Chinese subjects has passed from the ownership of the Earl of Wilton to that of Mr J. Pierpont Morgan.'

(Fig. 80) in the British Museum, painted with arms of Clifford, believed to be one of the earliest pieces of Chinese porcelain copied from an English silver design, suggests the outline of one of those early English silver coffee-pots with the spout at right angles to the handle. Chinese porcelain tea caddies of octagonal shape, resembling English silver models of Georgian date, trencher salts, whose shape is derived from silver trencher salts, fashionable in England about from 1695 until 1714, are common among export porcelain both in polychrome enamels and blue and white. It was during the reigns of Yung Chêng (1723–35) and Ch'ien Lung (1736–95) that most of the Chinese porcelain was copied from English silver models.

Porcelain decorated with European designs for the Western market covers a large family; of which the most important are the dinner, tea and coffee services; the jugs, salt-cellars and candlesticks decorated with European coats of arms.[1] The Chinese acquitted themselves well in the task of rendering the heraldic bearings given them to copy.

Some armorial porcelain goes back to the Ming period[2] and the earliest pieces are decorated in underglaze blue and white and usually carry coats of arms of Italian or Spanish families. It was not, however, until the reign of K'ang Hsi that the manufacture of heraldic services to orders transmitted by the Canton merchants became a regular feature of the trade. Tudor Craig gives the earliest date for these services as 1700.[3] The importance of these coats of arms in determining the date of manufacture has been pointed out by Hobson: 'An alliance which can be traced in Burke: a coronet or supporters indicating elevation to the peerage: a canton with a dexter hand gules, the emblem of a baronet: these and other unerring signs will often date an armorial service within a few years. A series of such pieces will supply

---

[1] This subject has been fully dealt with by the late Sir Algernon Tudor Craig in his *Armorial Porcelain of the Eighteenth Century*. Those who are interested should also refer to the catalogue of the Armorial Collection of the late Frederick Arthur Crisp, privately printed in 1907.

[2] The earliest piece in the Franks Collection at the British Museum is a bottle-shaped vase with flattened sides with blue and white decoration in the centre of which are the arms of Spain, copied from a dollar of either Philip II (1556–1598), Philip IV (1621–1665) or Charles II (1665–1700).

[3] In the Franks Collection there is a plate painted with the arms of De Vassy and inscribed 1702. A second plate exhibits the arms of Sir John Lambert who was created a baron in 1711 and died in 1722, so that the plate must have been made within those years. Other pieces of documentary interest are a tankard with the arms of Yorke impaling Cocks, an alliance which took place in 1720. Philip Yorke was created Baron Hardwicke in 1733, and the absence of supporters and a baron's coronet show that the plate must have been made between those years. A plate bearing the arms of James Laroche impaling those of Elizabeth Yeomans, must have been made between 1764 (the date of the alliance) and 1776 when James Laroche was created a baronet, as the insignia of the baronetcy are absent from the coat.

the whole history of the ware, besides giving many valuable hints on the classification of Chinese porcelain in general.'[1]

Until the beginning of the present century the mistaken idea that armorial china was the product of the English Lowestoft factory,[2] which flourished from 1757 to 1813, was quite common; according to another theory the porcelain was Chinese, but the decoration was carried out in England.

As the armorial designs were supplied from Europe and copied by the Chinese, certain errors are found in the armorial bearings, especially in the tinctures. This is due to the fact that often all the Chinese artist had to copy was an engraved bookplate; the tinctures being indicated in the usual way by vertical, horizontal and other lines. There are several instances of Chinese thoroughness, notably a service, on every piece of which, under the Arms, is the legend 'These are the Arms of myself and my wife' in a neat script, evidently an exact copy of a note on the original drawing. One of the rules of heraldry is that coloured charges must not be imposed on a coloured field or metal ones on a black background, but owing either to the ignorance of the owner or Chinese artists their rules were often broken. And the Chinese habit of depicting lions as kylins, which can be mistaken for heraldic tigers, has in at least one case caused a coat of arms to be assigned to the wrong family.[3]

Many dated pieces of armorial china have been preserved. A small bowl enamelled with the Derby Arms and inscribed 'Thomas Dear, Canton Anno domine 1770' was once in Tudor Craig's Collection.[4] Some of the moulds used to make European shapes are apparently still in existence at Ching-tê Chên today.[5]

In the British Museum there is a bill of lading (Fig. 70) addressed from Canton for the services made for Charles Peers in 1731 together with two examples of the services; one a plate in underglaze blue decorated with a pheasant on a rock amid flowering plants (Fig. 69) and the other a plate enamelled with the arms of the

[1] R. L. Hobson, 'On Some Armorial Porcelain in the Franks Collection', *The Connoisseur*, Vol. XXI, May-August 1908.

[2] Armorial bearings on export pieces indicate a date nearly fifty years antecedent to the formation of the Lowestoft factory. Chinese porcelain is of hard paste whereas the Lowestoft paste was the usual English soft paste till 1777.

[3] Tudor Craig, *Armorial Porcelain of the Eighteenth Century*.

[4] A pair of punch bowls (Crisp Collection) enamelled with the Hawkins Arms were inscribed and dated in the same way. A plate with the Chadwick Arms inscribed on the back 'Canton in China 24th Jan. 1791' was part of the service of which a plate is in the Franks Collection, British Museum.

[5] Mr Anthony Keswick recently ordered pieces for a dinner service from Ching-tê Chên to replace parts of a broken armorial service made for his family in China in the eighteenth century. From a minor imperfection it was possible to see that the sauce-boats had been made from the same mould as their eighteenth-century predecessors.

Peers family with panels of flowers set on the border in diaper pattern (Fig. 69).
A plate from the Okeover service is dated by a similar bill (1743), announcing the
consignment of four large dishes and fifty plates 'With your arms' to Leak Okeover.
From the invoice it can be seen that one of the services in question consisted of 524
pieces of which 312 were plates, and 56 dishes; the other pieces being salts, mugs,
sauce-boats, bowls, ewers and lavers.[1]

Various criteria as to the dating of undated armorial pieces have been advanced,
drawn from the designs of dated pieces. Thus the armorial of the K'ang Hsi period
in *famille verte* enamels is generally on a wide diapered border in *rouge de fer* and
gold, inset with small cartouches containing emblems and the shield of arms, is in
the 'Early English or Jacobean style'. Pieces decorated in the 'Imari' style in red,
blue and gold invariably belong to the early years of the eighteenth century, as also
those which are decorated in underglaze blue.

During the Yung-chêng period (1723–36) the borders of plates assume a more
open-work appearance; the flowers disappear from the back, and on some of the
services towards the end of the period the arms are shown in colour with a heavy
gold scroll border round the rim of the piece. It was during this period that the
decoration of the export porcelain seems to have shifted from Ching-tê-chên to
Canton. Originally orders were doubtless transmitted through Canton, and as the
porcelain was shipped from that town it soon occurred to the Cantonese that the
orders for special decorations could be conveniently carried out in the workshops in
Canton which were already engaged on the analogous work of painting on enamelled
metal.[2] Porcelain in the white was imported from Kiangsi for this purpose.

William Hickey, visiting Canton in 1768, describes these porcelain painting
shops. 'We were shown,' he writes, 'the different processes used in finishing the
China ware. In a long gallery we found upwards of a hundred persons at work in
sketching and finishing the various ornaments upon each particular piece of the ware,
some part of it being executed by men of advanced age and others by children which
were so young as six or seven years.'

On Honam Island, which divides the north-south channels of the Pearl River,
lying in midstream opposite the Shameen in the middle of Canton city, painting of
porcelain was still being carried out in similar sorting houses for foreign export in
1928. Most of the painters who sketched the design were men, and women filled in
the colours. Père d'Entrecolles classes the porcelain painters with ordinary workmen, and compares their efficiency to that of a European apprentice of four months

[1] The price charged is 228 taels (roughly the equivalent of £76).

[2] R. L. Hobson, *Guide to the Porcelain of the Far East* (British Museum Handbook), pp. 97 and 98.

standing; but he admits that these artists painted admirable flowers, animals, and landscapes on porcelain. Few artists who painted on porcelain or enamel ever signed their pieces, and when they did it is by a studio name, which does not identify them. The studio name Pai Shih (White Rock), sometimes combined with the cyclical year mark 1724, occurs on more than one of the Cantonese ruby-backed eggshell dishes, decorated with rockeries, peonies and cocks in bold outstanding colours.[1]

According to Bushell and Brinkley no porcelain decorated in underglaze blue was produced at Canton, and this is supported by Hobson. Pieces of export porcelain in which underglaze blue is combined with enamel colours are rare, although the coarse pieces of Chinese blue and white redecorated in Europe are not uncommon.

In the long reign of Ch'ien Lung several styles of design and *famille rose* decoration succeeded each other on armorial porcelain. From 1735 to 1753 the arms indicate the transitional period, and the decoration was inclined to be fairly plain with festoons or sprays of flowers and spearhead or cable designs round the rims. This was occasionally varied with exotic birds or small panels decorated with buildings and shipping scenes, indicating the port of departure, journey and destination of the china itself (Fig. 79).[2] From about 1750 to 1770 the frame of the arms is in the rococo style. This was followed about 1770 by the arms being contained in spade-shaped shields, wreathed with festoons of flowers, until about 1785, when the perfectly plain spade-shaped shield began to appear with dark blue borders round the rims dotted with gold stars. From 1795 until about 1810 armorial china is almost always decorated with wide diapered circles in deep blue. The arms were still painted in their proper colours.

Sometimes the connections of an English family are recorded for several generations on their imported services. The Roberts family[3] had one service made in the reign of Yung Chêng about 1735, and another in 1780 (Roberts with Fenton in pretence), and a third about 1795 (Bowden impaling Roberts). Many high officials of the East India Company and several Lord Mayors had services emblazoned with the arms of the company, and the great city companies also patronized armorial wares. Services were made for the Bakers' Company about 1760; the Butchers' Company about 1750; the Fishmongers' about 1775; and pieces exist with the arms of the Clothiers' Company and the Blacksmiths' Company. One of the earliest of

[1] There is sufficient evidence to show that these plates, especially the ones with elaborate borders, were exported in sets to Europe, and it is only breakage which has reduced their number and made them the rarities they are today (see Appendix).

[2] Tudor Craig, *Armorial Porcelain of the Eighteenth Century*, pp. 8 and 9.

[3] Tudor Craig, *op. cit.*, p. 13.

these services (made for the Poulterers' Company about 1745) carries the motto 'Remember your oath'.

Light feathery scrolls, gilt or in colours, rococo ornaments with floral patterns and the scroll-edged frames of lattice work, which were typical of the early Ch'ien Lung period, are also characteristic. The bulk of these export porcelains are usually distinguished by their washy pink enamel, which contrasts with the thick carmine of the early *famille rose*, and by their coarse grey and white bodies. Pieces of this nature, including those decorated with peacocks at regular intervals, generally in black and gold, date from 1740 to 1760. Composite bodies with diapers, symbols, flowers and butterflies, half Chinese and half European, range from 1765 to 1820. In the last decades of the century 'such purely European borders as the swags of flowers used at Bow and Bristol; the floral and laurel wreaths and husk festoons; the pink scale patterns of Meissen; ribbons and dotted lines winding through a floral band, feather scrolls, of Sèvres origin',[1] were in fashion, and also blue borders with gilt edges and gilt stars and the corn-flower sprigs of the French hard-paste porcelains. The export of armorial wares to England from China ceases soon after 1800, perhaps because the Worcester factory had by that time established its own manufacture of armorial services. The tariff was too high to allow the trade to continue.[2] But an advertisement (1804) gives the name of a China merchant who was still prepared to supply the American market.[3]

A number of export pieces decorated with European subjects includes the so-called 'Jesuit' China, a name commonly applied to Chinese porcelain decorated with Christian subjects. This ware is thus described by Père d'Entrecolles (writing in 1712): 'From the debris at a large emporium they brought me a little plate, which I treasure more than the finest porcelain made during the last thousand years. In the centre of the plate is painted a crucifix between the Virgin and St John, and I am told that this kind of porcelain was shipped sometimes to Japan, but that this commerce came to an end sixteen or seventeen years ago. Apparently the Japanese Christians took advantage of the manufacture at the time of the persecution to

---

[1] R. L. Hobson, 'On Some Armorial Porcelain in the Franks Collection', *The Connoisseur*, Vol. XXI, May–August 1908.

[2] In 1803 a proposal to reduce the import duty on Oriental porcelain by £59 8s. 6d. per cent (which would have left a mere 50 per cent duty to be paid) was regarded with alarm by the Staffordshire potters. F. Falkner, *The Wood Family of Burslem*.

[3] 'Yam Shinqua, China ware merchant, Canton, Begs leave respectfully to inform American merchants super-cargoes, and captains, that he promises to be manufactured in the best possible manner all sorts of China ware with Arms, Cyphers and other decorations (if required) on the most reasonable terms, dated June 8th, 1804.' Gertrude S. Kimball, *The East Indies Trade of Providence*.

obtain pictures of our mysteries, and these wares mingled with others in the crates evaded the vigilance of the enemies of our religion. This pious artifice was no doubt eventually discovered and rendered useless by more stringent investigations, and that is why the manufacture of this kind of ware has ceased at Ching-tê Chên.'[1] Earliest examples are painted in underglaze blue, the Christian designs being accompanied by Chinese ornaments.[2] A bowl with a fungus mark on the base in the Franks Collection at the British Museum has a Crucifixion on the exterior framed in a pattern of cloud scrolls, and inside a Buddhist seal symbol in flames and clouds (Fig. 86). This and another cup in the collection which has a jade mark on the base, and a Crucifixion half lost among surrounding scrolls are both of the K'ang Hsi period, and were probably painted at Ching-tê Chên; and, as their general style indicates that they were for Oriental use, may well have been made, D'Entrecolles suggests, as export to Japan.

After an interval Christian motives reappear in the Yung Chêng period. The Yung Chêng pieces, which are more sophisticated in form and usually in black monochrome touched with gold, were probably the work of Canton decorators. The designs are chiefly copied from European engravings, although the hatched lines employed are different from any sort of print, and the Chinese translation of these originals gives a strong impression of parody or burlesque. They were not made for the use of missionaries but for export. A plate in the British Museum collection represents Christ rising from the tomb, under which sits an angel. On the ground lie four soldiers stretched in sleep; while there is a fifth in the background; in the distance three little figures are watching the miracle (Fig. 85).

The Crucifixion and other Christian subjects reappear again in Ch'ien Lung's reign on plates decorated with highly coloured enamels.[3]

In some of these pieces the effect of engraving is imitated by delicate and accurate brush strokes, in others the surface is cut by a fine tool and ink rubbed into the strokes.

[1] Quoted by Hobson, *Chinese Pottery and Porcelain*, Vol. II, pp. 252 and 253.

[2] 'An early (to judge from the general style of the piece, late Ming) example is a pear-shaped ewer, with elongated spout and handle, in the Kunstgewerbe Museum, Berlin. On the side is the sacred monogram I.H.S. surrounded by formal ornaments, and it has been plausibly said that the little vessel has been used for Communion purposes.' Hobson, *Chinese Pottery and Porcelain*, Vol. II, p. 252.

[3] A plate in red and gold in the British Museum collection has a central medallion motif adapted from an engraving of the baptism of Christ. 'The two actors in the scene are represented as wild Orientals, the acrobatic attitude of the baptizing figure being especially remarkable. In the air is the Holy Dove and from it depends a collection of streamers, whose value in the original engraving can scarcely be conjectured. On the border are four strange looking nude children with wings, doubtless representing angels. Two of them hold a basket of flowers, and two a scroll lettered "Math. 3.16."' William King, 'Jesuit China,' *Country Life*, June 7th, 1930.

In two fine dishes (Figs. 88 and 89) the Chinese artist has imitated the print so carefully that at first glance the dishes appear as if decorated by transfer printing, a process never employed by the Chinese. Each dish carries the coat of arms of Luns-ford on the back. One dish, representing Thetis dipping the infant Achilles in the Styx, has a label on the back 'a 16-in. circular dish of Oriental China finely painted in *grisaille* with the immersion of Achilles after Le Suer (*sic*)'. This dish is painted chiefly in black, but on its companion, which represents the Triumph of Mordecai arrayed in royal apparel riding through the city preceded by Haman, gilding is a part of the design.

Next to the imperial factory at Ching-tê Chên the largest ceramic centre was that of the Tê-hua factory in Fukien province where the so-called *Blanc de chine* figures and wares were made. One of the most common of the former are representations of the Buddhist goddess of mercy, Kuan yin.[1] She is frequently depicted in a maternal aspect and her resemblance to the Christian Madonna was exploited to the full by the early Jesuit missionaries. Numbers of these Kuan yin which have survived in Europe have been lacquered in red.

Some of the earliest pieces of export porcelain are decorated entirely in underglaze blue, such as the tall cups with covers decorated with panels containing St Louis of France and his Queen and inscribed round the top '*L'Empire de la vertu est établi jusqu'au bout de l'univers*' (Fig. 81). Though this ware must have used or adapted Western designs or prints, it is rare to trace their sources. A punch bowl is painted with Hogarth's *Calais Gate* (1761) and a plate decorated with Picart's *Pèlerins de L'isle de Cithère* follows an engraving (dated 1708). Instructions to Dutch merch-ants in China, referring to a chest containing new and fashionable designs, are quoted in de Vries.[2]

The range of export art included subjects of political and topical interest. En-gravings of the Duke of Cumberland, Prince Charles Edward (the Young Pre-tender) (Fig. 105), and John Wilkes[3] were all rendered on mugs and punch bowls for the British market with appropriate sentiments inscribed under them. Sporting (Fig. 96) and harvest scenes, ships with views of famous anchorages and pictures of the 'hongs' at Canton, and services with European horticultural subjects also exist. Dutch skippers made a practice of ordering pictures of their ships to be

[1] She was also a goddess of fertility and patron of seafarers.

[2] de Vries, *Porselein, Chineesch en Europeesch Porselein*, 1923, pp. 12, 13.

[3] A punch bowl in the British Museum (Fig. 97) is decorated with a bust of John Wilkes with the motto 'always ready in a good cause' and inscribed above 'Wilkes and Liberty'; and a bust of Lord Mansfield with the Motto: 'Justice sans Pitie.'

painted on plates when detained in harbour. Jacquemart mentions the picture of such a vessel inscribed underneath in Dutch 'The ship Vryburg conducted by Captain Jacob Ryzik in China in the year 1756'. A plate with a ship in the Franks collection is inscribed in Dutch 'Christopher Schooneman, chief mate of the ship Vryburg, in the roads off Whampoo in China in the year 1736' (Fig. 99).

As the Dutch were the largest importers of Oriental porcelain at the beginning of the eighteenth century, the largest body of European-decorated Chinese porcelain comes from Holland. The decoration of Chinese wares imported in the white was begun in the early years of the eighteenth century by the Dutch. Gersaint, in his catalogue published in Paris in 1747, describes two bottles in which figures, animals, and other ornaments 'have been painted in Holland as is done there often very *mal à propos* on pieces of fine white porcelain'.[1] The Dutch red is nearly always distinctive, being of a brick-red tint, piled on and imperfectly glazed. In 1755 Gerrit van der Kaade opened a shop exclusively for the sale of Dutch enamelled Oriental porcelain, and it was from this and similar shops that factory owners recruited enamellers. One of the earliest dated pieces of this Dutch decoration is a Chinese plate in the British Museum enamelled with a sailing vessel bearing the arms of Zeeland and the date 1700 on the stern (Fig. 98).[2] The hot red-brown and light blue enamel of the Dutch decorators can be easily detected. The bulk of these Dutch-decorated Chinese pieces[3] although frequently catalogued and sold as Chinese, are covered with designs in the style and palette associated with the Japanese potter Kakiemon (Fig. 100).

Decoration of Chinese wares was seldom attempted in Italy or France. In a paper on *German and English Decorators of Chinese Porcelain*[4] reproductions are given of the work of Daniel Preissler (1636–1733) (Fig. 107) and his son Ignaz Preissler, who worked in Friedrichswalde in Silesia near the Bohemian border, and at Kronstadt in Bohemia itself. The son, according to contemporary correspondence, was in the habit of painting on 'Chinese porcelain with blue borders'. Ignaz Bottengruber of Breslau worked in red monochrome on similar pieces and J. Metzich, one of the

[1] The Dutch were not averse to painting Chinese pieces already slightly decorated in underglaze blue. Small white cups from Têhua were often favoured for decoration.

[2] See W. W. Winkworth, 'The Delft Enamellers', *Burlington Magazine*, June 1928, p. 296, and W. B. Honey, 'Dutch Decorations on Chinese Porcelains,' *Antiques*, February 1932, p. 75.

[3] Neither the enamels nor the designs were exactly copied by the Dutch decorators, but their influence is obvious. One of the designs favoured by the Dutch is of parrots; a design which has been called 'the cherry pickers' is also a favourite.

[4] W. B. Honey, *Antiques*, March 1932, pp. 125 *et seq.*

Bayreuth *hausmaler*, apparently used pieces of Yung Chêng porcelain of fine quality to paint upon. It is not until about 1750 that there is evidence of the existence of English enamelling shops likely to have used Chinese porcelain. Several pieces decorated in England have been associated with the name of James Giles, a London enameller with a show-room in Cockspur Street and later in Berwick Street, Soho; and with one O'Neale (or O'Neil), a miniature painter who is recorded as casually employed at Chelsea between 1770–1773.

In the late eighteenth and early nineteenth century the name of Thomas Baxter has been associated with the redecoration of certain cups, dishes and tea caddies with gilt bands and borders.

The term 'clobbered ware'[1] has been applied to all pieces of Oriental porcelain which were redecorated in Europe, but it is perhaps best reserved for the crude pieces of Chinese blue and white which were smothered in green, pink, yellow and green enamels in England during the nineteenth century.

[1] The British Museum possesses a bottle of fine K'ang Hsi porcelain decorated with monsters in underglaze copper red, with an additional figure and foliage painted in enamel by the Dutch which is a very superior piece of clobbering if one accepts the wider definition of the term (Fig. 109).

CHAPTER V

PAINTED (CANTON) ENAMELS

THE process of painting in enamels on metal is a simple one. The surface to be decorated is covered with an even coating of opaque enamel, and the design painted in enamel colours on this as on porcelain. In China the origin of this technique is indicated by the Chinese name *Yang Tzu* (foreign porcelain) for these wares.

The date of the introduction of painted enamels into China has not hitherto been recorded, although it has been stated by M. Soulié de Morant that foreign missionaries had brought in the technique as early as 1685.[1] From an unpublished letter dated 1720, from de Mailla, a French missionary in China, it is clear that the Emperor K'ang Hsi had become acquainted with European painted enamels before 1713, either through the medium of the French missionaries at Peking, or by traders at Canton; and that in 1713 or 1714 he set up an atelier at Peking for the manufacture of enamels. When Brother Gravereau, a French missionary who was skilled in painted enamels, arrived at Pekin in 1719 in response to an appeal from the mission at Peking, it was found that the Chinese artists had made some progress during the interval. (See Appendix A.)

The vase (Fig. 113) if not by a European hand may easily have been made under Jesuit influence. It is decorated with a landscape containing several churches; the trees are not painted in the usual Chinese style, while the sky is a bright cerulean blue (it is intentionally left white on Chinese pieces); but this piece may be by a Chinese hand working under European influence.

Ferguson, who distinguishes between enamels painted at Peking and those painted at Canton, writes that the Peking enamels were 'made after the model of Limoges pieces brought to China by Catholic missionaries. A few of the missionaries themselves were skilled in enamel painting, and they trained Chinese artists. Some of

[1] Soulié de Morant, *Histoire de l'art Chinois*, p. 23. He states that painted enamels were made in Peking between 1685 and 1719 for the *'Compagnie de la Chine'*. *'Le décor'* (he adds) *'est frais, très fin, et délicat.'* He suggests the year 1683 as the first date of manufacture at Canton.

these pieces are copies or adaptations of those brought from France and have persons in foreign dress and backgrounds. Others have familiar Chinese designs . . . the enamels painted at Canton are inferior in quality to those formerly made in the *Tsao Pan Ch'u* of the Peking Palace. Canton enamels have been made in large quantities chiefly for foreign export and are still being produced, but they cannot be classed among artistic wares.'[1] Perhaps he had in his mind the opinion of the author of the *Wên Fang Ssŭ K'ao* (published in 1782) whose depreciation of painted enamel has often been applied incorrectly to cloisonné. 'One often sees,' he says, 'incense urns and flower vases, wine cups and saucers, bowls and dishes, ewers for wine, and round boxes for cake and fruit, painted in very brilliant colours; but, although vulgarly called porcelain, these things have nothing of the pure translucency of true porcelain. They are only fit for use as ornaments of ladies' apartments—not at all for the chaste furniture or the library of a simple scholar.'[2]

Canton enamel continued to be classed as a species of 'foreign' porcelain, in works devoted to Chinese ceramics, but it is usually distinguished by Chinese writers from cloisonné and champlevé enamels.

Thus the *Ching-tê Chên T'ao Lu*[3] divides porcelain with copper bodies into *Ta Shi Yao* (Porcelain of the Arab); *Fa Lang Yao* (Porcelain of France) and *Yang T'zu Yao* (Foreign porcelain ware). The first two groups appear to refer to cloisonné and champlevé enamels and the last to painted enamels. The passage under the heading of *Yang tz'u yao* (foreign porcelain ware) runs: 'It is made in the land of Kuli[4] in the Western ocean. The origin of the ware has not yet been investigated. In like manner (to the cloisonné enamel) it has a copper body. This is very thinly coated with *tz'u fên* (powder made of porcelain stone) which is fired. When complete it has brilliant paintings in enamels (*wu sê* "five colour") admirably executed. When struck it emanates a note like copper. In glossiness, elegance, freshness, beauty it is really not equal to porcelain wares. At the present in Kwang-tung imitations are made in great numbers.'[5]

In the catalogue of the exhibition of pieces from the Palace Collections sent over to London by the Chinese government in 1936, Volume II, which deals with porcelain, includes seven pieces of Canton enamel (Nos. 300–306) illustrated between porcelain described in the catalogue as painted in 'cloisonné enamels', and other

[1] John C. Ferguson, *Survey of Chinese Art*, pp. 128 and 129.
[2] Quoted in Bushell, *Chinese Art*, Vol. II, p. 85.
[3] Published in 1815.
[4] Calcutta.
[5] Stanislas Julien, *Histoire et fabrication de la porcelaine Chinoise*, p. 37.

pieces described as 'cloisonné enamels on glass'; five other painted enamel pieces (three of which are enamelled on a gold body) are reproduced in Vol. IV in the Miscellaneous Section, which is devoted to cloisonné. It is difficult to understand why this division was made.

The similarity of decoration and enamel colouring between the painted enamels on copper and those of contemporary pieces of eggshell porcelain, particularly on some of the ruby-backed plates, has often been noticed. Dishes occur in the two materials with the identical ruby backs and the same brocade patterns and diaper borders, interrupted by foliate panels filled with the same devices. The figure subjects in Chinese interiors, the groups of furniture and vases of formal flowers, the intricate diapers of the borders and the ruby backs of the dishes typical of the eggshell porcelain appear also on the Canton enamels. As 'it is practically certain that most of the well-known class of eggshell porcelains, such wares as the "seven-bordered plates" and the "ruby-backed" dishes, if not all of it, though made at Ching-tê Chên, was enamelled at Canton',[1] it is probable that many of their pieces were made in the same atelier by the same decorators.

The enamels on the hard porcelain glaze stand out in relief like incrustations.[2] On the other hand the colours of Canton enamels are painted on a ground of opaque enamel, usually white. It is like painting on the tin-enamelled surface of Delft, or to a lesser degree on the easily fusible glaze of 'soft paste' porcelain. The colours sink in and are incorporated with the soft excipient, and assume a softer appearance. As some of the colours do not do themselves justice on the enamel excipient the Chinese verdict that 'in glossiness, elegance, freshness and beauty, they (viz. the Canton enamels) cannot equal the porcelain wares' can be justified. It is unfortunate that they easily crack and chip.

Canton enamels often carry dynastic marks on the base; the *nien-hao* of Ch'ien Lung being the most common. More rarely 'hall-marks' or marks of commendation appear; often in seal characters.[3] One looks in vain for pieces signed by their enamellers.

[1] R. L. Hobson, 'A Note on Canton Enamels', *Burlington Magazine*, Vol. XXII, Dec. 1912, pp. 165–167.

[2] 'The enamel colours used in Canton are well known from analyses by Ebelmen and Salvetat of a collection actually taken from the palette of an enameller, while he was working at his table, by a French attaché in the year 1844 and published in the *Recueil des Travaux Scientifiques* (M. Ebelman), Vol. I, p. 377. S. Bushell, *Chinese Art*, Vol. II, p. 84.

[3] e.g. *Ch'ing Wan* (Pure trinket); *Ch'ing Wan t'ang* (Ch'ing Wan hall); *Wên Kung t'ang* (Hall of General Inquiry); *ju i* (as you wish).

Studio marks occur on certain pieces. 'The name Pai Shih,[1] usually in seal form and attached to a stanza of poetry or a short descriptive sentence, occurs fairly frequently on Canton enamels, but always (as in the eggshell plate [2] quoted by Bushell) in the decoration and never under the base. The latter is the proper and usual place for the pattern mark or painter's signature on porcelain or enamel; the former is a quite usual place in a picture for the signature of the artist. . . . I am convinced that Pai Shih was merely the name of a Canton artist, whose pictures were freely used by the enamellers; he may even have designed specially for them. There is no uniformity of style in the Pai Shih pieces.'[3] The signature has been found on eggshell porcelain plates painted with elaborate finish with masses of flowers and borders of the 'seven border' style. The same signature will be found in Canton enamels usually attached to a landscape, sometimes well painted, but sometimes rendered in a rough and sketchy style. 'It would have been much more satisfactory had the signature of Pai Shih been that of a porcelain and enamel-painter and so served definitely to bring the two materials under one roof; but the theory must be dismissed and with it the significance of the date 1724 attached to a Pai Shih painting on porcelain. It is no longer considered the date of the porcelain but of the design only.'[4]

In some pieces it is their decorative motives, entirely alien to China, which betray that they have been made for the foreign market; in others the shape shows their export origin. This is evident in the kettle standing on a stand (Fig. 114) which must have been made for the English market about 1760, as the shape has been taken from contemporary English silver.

By the end of the reign of Ch'ien Lung (1796) Canton enamels had lost all their quality of colour and design. By the nineteenth century they were decadent 'but still manufactured in large quantities at Hoihow in Hainan, generally on a silver body. Pale blue is now the dominant colour, the decoration is simple'. There were also pieces made in black enamel, which probably came from the same port.

[1] 'White Stone.'

[2] The porcelain plate in question is of the ruby-backed eggshell family, painted with quails with an inscription *Ling nan hua chi* (painted at Canton), accompanied by the studio name Pai Shih.

[3] R. L. Hobson, *Burlington Magazine*, December 1912 (Vol. XXII, pp. 165–167).

[4] R. L. Hobson, *Burlington Magazine*, December 1912 (Vol. XXII, pp. 165–167).

CHAPTER VI

CARVING IN IVORY
TORTOISESHELL
AND MOTHER-OF-PEARL

BESIDES the major imports from China there were curious trifles which met the European demand for objects displaying intricate craftsmanship. Among these were carved ivory fan sticks, patterned and perforated concentric spheres of ivory, and models of junks, temples and pagodas, in ivory, mother-of-pearl and sandalwood.

Laufer[1] states, without giving his authority, that 'patterned and perforated balls were manufactured as early as the fourteenth century under the name of "devils' work balls" ' adding 'there is a tradition also that they were made in the palace of the Sung Emperors'.

A full account of some intricate ivory toys is to be found in John Barrow's *Travels in China* (1804). He speaks of the perfection of Chinese ivory cutting. 'Of all the mechanical arts that in which they seem to have attained the highest degree of perfection is the cutting of ivory.[2] Nothing can be more exquisitely beautiful than the fine openwork displayed in a Chinese fan, the sticks of which would seem to be singly cut by the hand; for whatever pattern may be required, a shield with a coat of arms, or a cypher, the article will be finished according to the drawing at the shortest notice. The two outside sticks are full of bold sharp work, undercut in such a manner as could not be performed in any other way than by the hand. In short,' he continues, 'all kinds of toys for children and other trinkets and trifles are executed in a similar manner and for less money in China than in any other part of the world. Out of a solid ball of ivory, with a hole in it not more than an inch in diameter, they will cut from nine to fifteen distinct hollow globes, one within another, all loose and

---

[1] Berthold Laufer, 'Ivory in China', *Field Museum of Natural History*, Chicago, 1925.

[2] 'In this trade they stand unparalleled even at Birmingham, that great nursery of the art of manufacture where I understand it has been attempted by means of a machine to cut ivory fans and other articles, in imitation of those of the Chinese, but this experiment, although ingenious, has not hitherto succeeded to that degree so as to produce articles fit to vie with those of the latter.'

capable of being turned round in every direction and each of them carved full of the same kind of openwork that appears on the fans. A very small sum of money is the price of these trifles.'[1] Later in the nineteenth century these 'true Chinese puzzles which foil the efforts of the Fanquis to discover the work of constructing them', with other ivory carvings, could be bought as cheaply in England as in China, as the market had been for a long time overloaded.[2] These concentric balls, marvels of technical ingenuity, are usually assigned to the nineteenth century.

Canton, Amoy, Shanghai, Soochow and Peking were and are all centres of the ivory industry, and as a rule the objects are still carved and sold in the shops in which they were made. Canton, since the earliest years of foreign contact with China, has produced the bulk of the immense quantities of ivory carvings. Bushell points out that in 1680, among the twenty-six ateliers established in the Tso Pan Chu within the palace was one devoted to ivory carvings. This atelier closed down after the reign of Ch'ien Lung.

Among the ivory objects made by the Chinese are combs, back-scratchers (often of walrus ivory), dice, chop-sticks, statuettes, snuff bottles, brush holders, arm rests, stems and mouthpieces of opium pipes, boxes to hold opium and spatulas to handle it, chessmen, fan handles, dominoes, the tops of cricket cages, archers' rings, tubes for peacock feathers in Mandarin hats, and various kinds of girdle ornaments and per-fume boxes. Many of the articles are dyed green with verdigris and the cheaper ones pink. These objects were not made for the European market, although some of them found their way to England as curiosities in the eighteenth century. The concentric balls, brooches, chains, glove and other boxes, fans, counters and fish for gambling, and architectural models, were made for the foreign market. Bushell[3] illustrates a group of pavilions, carved in ivory and partly coloured, set in an ornamental garden enlivened with small figures of Chinese men and women. The principal pavilion is two-storied, with pillared verandahs and trellised walls. On the roof is a flaming jewel and fish-dragons which project from the angles of the eaves. Another model is of a Buddhist temple poised on the slope of a rocky hill which is set with small pavilions, pagodas, gates and hedges carved in ivory, and with trees of gilded metal with blossom of coral and jewels; the storks in the garden are shaped in mother-of-pearl, and the small ponds are worked in the same material. These were part of other set pieces sent by the Emperor of China to Josephine, wife

[1] John Barrow, *Travels in China* (1804), pp. 308–9. (Barrow was private secretary to Lord Macartney on his mission to China in 1792.)

[2] Douning, *The Fanquis in China* (1838), Vol. 2, p. 67.

[3] Bushell, *Chinese Art* (ed. 1924), Vol. I. Plate opposite p. 105.

of Napoleon Bonaparte, then first Consul, and captured by an English ship of war on the way to Europe. After the Treaty of Amiens in 1802 the restitution of these presents was offered, but declined.

Among the ivories imported to Europe are numbers of carved chessmen. Both chess[1] and backgammon pieces were made in ivory in China from an early period. Speaking of the elaborately carved ivory chess sets exported from China to Europe, Murray, in his *History of Chess*, writes: 'These are something quite different from the inscribed counters which are the sole type of man used in the native game and obviously not intended for use in the native chess, since the set consists of a King, Queen, two priests or mandarins, two horsemen, two castles (elephants with flags on their backs) and eight soldiers on each side. It is evident that these sets (which commonly represent Chinese on one side and Mongols on the other) are only the result of an attempt to treat the European chessmen from a Chinese point of view.' These Chinese chess pieces are of no value for the history of chess. They merely illustrate that popularity of chess in Europe which created a market for curious implements of play.[2] Most of these sets are not earlier than the nineteenth century.

Sandalwood was often carved almost as delicately as ivory and possesses nearly as much hardness and durability.[3] Canton also exported works in tortoiseshell[4] and horn. These two substances lend themselves to the same carved technique; both are softened by water and heat, and then stretched, bent, split apart and moulded. Fans, workboxes and ornaments in tortoiseshell were imported by the West in the eighteenth century. The commonest objects are the small round toilet boxes having the outside of the lid and sides deeply undercut with processions of mandarins riding on horseback holding state umbrellas over their heads, and accompanied by attendants on foot, in a landscape diversified with bridges, pagodas and *pai lou* (gateways), often inscribed with felicitous hall names.[5] The tortoiseshell boxes (Fig. 133) are

[1] Chess, like backgammon, is a game of Indian origin which reached China either directly from India, or from Persia, through Chinese Turkestan, during the Wei dynasty (A.D. 220–260). The Chinese name for it is 'Siang k'i' which can be translated 'the Elephant Game' or 'the Ivory game'. Jesuits brought the first knowledge of it to Europe together with sets of the pieces in the sixteenth century. The most important Chinese classic on the subject is *The Secrets of the Orange Grove*, a Chinese work dating from 1632. In the *Shosoin* Repository in Japan there is a backgammon board of sandalwood inlaid with ivory and an ivory measure painted in red and green which go back to the T'ang dynasty.

[2] H. I. R. Murray, *History of Chess*, p. 134.

[3] Douning, *The Fanquis in China*, 1838, Vol. II, p. 70.

[4] The shell of the loggerhead turtle (*Chelonea Imbricata*), a native of the Malay Archipelago and the Indian Ocean.

[5] These same motives occur on the carved ivory boxes.

often mounted in gold. Tortoiseshell ware continued to be exported in the nine-teenth century and 'various fancy articles' are mentioned as exported in considerable quantities to all parts of the world in 1847.[1]

Canton was also the centre of the manufacture of carved rhinoceros horn cups[2] which were known in China as early as the Han dynasty. Rhinoceros horn cups and cornucopias, carved in openwork (usually with Taoist designs deeply undercut), were exported all over the near East in the eighteenth century and some of them drifted to Europe (Fig. 130).

Carved jade was not bought by Europe in any quantities, although Canton was from the eighteenth century onwards the headquarters of the industry in green Burmese jade. Probably the material was too expensive for the European market. But many pieces of carved soapstone, a cheaper substitute for jade, reached Europe in the eighteenth century. Several of these came to the British Museum with the Sloane Collection (Fig. 128). A few pieces of Chinese pewter and glass must have reached Europe in the same way.

Nearly all accounts of cargoes imported from China from the middle of the eighteenth century onwards include large quantities of mother-of-pearl. Peter Osbeck (who visited Canton between 1750 and 1752 in the Swedish East India Company's three-decker *Prince Charles*) speaks of the return cargo as containing 2,165 pounds of mother-of-pearl and also buttons,[3] and Phipps,[4] listing the chief articles of the China Trade in 1834, mentions gold, silver, ivory and tortoiseshell ware and 266,000 pounds of mother-of-pearl. It is difficult to surmise what these vast quantities of mother-of-pearl were used for. Large numbers of engraved mother-of-pearl counters, some of them in the shape of fish, which were used for gambling, have survived. Most of the mother-of-pearl inlay in early Victorian furniture must have come from this source.

[1] R. M. Martin, *China, political, commercial and social* (1847), Vol. II, p. 124.

[2] Both from the one-horned Indian and two-horned Sumatra rhinoceros. Not only were rhinoceros horns credited with prophylactic powers, but they were supposed to record the presence of poison by an exudation of a white humour.

[3] Peter Osbeck, *A Voyage to China and the East Indies*, 1750–1752.

[4] *China and Eastern Trade*, 1835.

CHAPTER VII

SILK TEXTILES

FOR more than three thousand years the Chinese have been accustomed to weave textile fabrics, and in silk fabrics they had the natural advantage of their early skill and monopoly of sericulture. During the late years of the seventeenth century, quantities of woven, embroidered and painted silks were shipped to Europe, and this export reached its widest extension during the eighteenth century, competing in the European market by their decorative colour and charm of design. The vogue in England for Chinese silks was widespread, the general fancy of the people 'running upon East India goods' and 'even the Queen herself at this time (i.e. 1708) was pleased to appear in China and Japan—China silks and calico'.[1] Yielding to the pressure of manufacturers, the government in 1700 forbade the use of wrought silks made in India, Persia or China.[2]

In France, where the silk-weaving industry was of major importance, efforts were made by finance ministers to control and to reduce the influx of oriental silks. In 1686 Louvois issued an order forbidding the importation of painted silks from the East.[3] In certain eighteenth-century French silks there is evidence of a new direction in design from Chinese fabrics; and the number of Chinese silk damasks copied or adapted from European designs of the sixteenth and seventeenth centuries points to European influence.

Even in the middle years of the seventeenth century 'great quantities of silk stuffs were brought from China'.[4] The immense production of silk in China is noted by travellers in the eighteenth century. Le Comte writes that silk was made in many provinces, but that 'the best and fairest is to be found in that of Chekian (Chekiang). The traffick of it is so great that this province alone is able to supply all

[1] *Weekly Review*, 1708.

[2] *Statutes*, XII, 598.

[3] H. Cordier, *La Chine en France au XVIIIme siècle* (1910, pp. 48–9).

[4] 'Great quantities of silk stuffs were brought from China and sold at very low rates.' *State Papers, Domestic*, 1639–40, p. 35.

China and the greatest part of Europe'.[1] Savary des Bruslons also speaks of the province as this 'greatest producer of silk in the world, producing as much as all Europe and Asia combined'. The margin of profit made by Western merchants was immense.

In France the silk industry of Lyons was supreme in Europe, and in consequence sensitive to the effect of imported silks on the market. In 1792 deputies from the city complained of the damage caused by the great influx of East Indian and Chinese goods.

The textiles chiefly exported to Europe were brocades and damasks and also embroidered silks and satins. Permission was given in 1677 to factors, writers, owners of ships, officers and seamen of the English East India Company's ships to bring home 'from the Indies' all sorts of flowered silks from China'.[2] The instructions given to the East India Company's supercargoes of the ship *Dorothy* (sent to Amoy in 1694) include a list of articles which were held suitable for the English market, such as silks, damasks, satins, velvets (plain, flowered and embroidered). In the late eighteenth century the principal silk stuffs manufactured by the Chinese are stated to be 'plain and flowered gauzes, damasks of all colours, striped and black satins, clouded and pinked taffetas, crapes, brocades, plush and plain and different kinds of velvet'. Velvet-weaving does not seem to have been practised in China before the Ming period, and the knowledge of this technique may have reached China from the West. Tapestry (*K'o-ssu*) woven with silk and gold thread 'identical with that by which the European tapestries are produced, except in the greater fineness of the texture, and in the frequent use of the brush for subordinate features of the design',[3] was not made for export.

Silk, when exposed to sunlight, is a perishable fabric, and though silk curtains and hangings are often mentioned[4] in the eighteenth century, few have survived (Fig. 140). Specimens of Chinese woven fabrics still existing have usually been preserved in the form of wrappings for relics or materials for vestments (Fig. 135). A piece of light red damask, having a circular design of cranes, interspersed with sprays of pomegranates, in the church of Asbo in Ostergotland must date from at least 1697, on the evidence of the European embroidery bearing this date. A red

---

[1] *Remarks made on about ten years travel through the Empire of China* (trans., 1737, p. 138).

[2] October 19th, 1677. *Court Minutes of the East India Company*, 1677–79.

[3] *Brief guide to the Chinese woven fabrics*, Victoria and Albert Museum, ed. 1938, p. 18.

[4] At Wanstead in 1722, the antechamber was 'furnished with china silk, stained in colours, incomparably fine', the bedchamber, dressing rooms and closet all also of China silk. J. Macky, *Journey Through England*, 1722, Vol. I.

silk hanging, embroidered in China with a dragon, kylins and Immortals, is known to have been given in 1705 to the church of Gottröra in Upland, also in Sweden.

Chinese embroideries were not only made for the general European market, but also in response to the orders of private individuals, who were able to use the medium of the East India trading companies. Bed furniture and bed-covers were imported in large numbers into Western Europe during the late seventeenth and early eighteenth centuries. In a bed cover of red silk embroidered in coloured silks and gold thread, preserved at Hatfield, the design centres in a medallion embroidered with galloping horses; and the surrounding area with kylins and stylized floral ornament. There is a broad border worked with flowers and birds in flight (Fig. 143). A medallion embroidered in coloured silks on a yellow silk ground (part of a bed-cover) can be dated by its armorial medallion, which is blazoned with the arms of the Duke of Chandos, impaling those of his second wife, Cassandra Willoughby. The creation of the Dukedom of Chandos in 1719 and the death of the Duchess in 1735, give terminal dates for this embroidery[1] (Fig. 142).

As a result of the low cost of production in China embroidered garments were shipped to Europe, and garments cut to the required size and shape were also dispatched to China to be embroidered. Saint-Aubin speaks with enthusiasm of Chinese embroidery in silk as unrivalled for its regularity and finish.[2] 'The varied direction of their stitches, the extreme cleanliness and care of the Chinese embroiders preserve the lustre and freshness of their work.' 'There is no country where work is carried on with such cleanliness, and so cheaply.' In his day embroideries worked with fine and evenly whipped cords came into fashion. 'This (he says) we owe to the Chinese, by whom many embroideries most precise in regularity have been made for our dandies.' In 1751, Mrs Montagu mentions sending to China some white satin flounces to be embroidered in white.[3] The most usual ground for Chinese embroideries is silk, but English broadcloth, especially the military scarlet, was much liked in China as a basis for embroidery. As a result of the conservatism of Chinese craftsmen and designers, the same patterns were produced for a long period.

[1] James Brydges, Lord Chandos, was created Duke of Chandos in 1719. The armorial medallion is surrounded by floral ornament and pots of flowers symmetrically arranged.

[2] *Description des arts et métiers*, Vol. XI (*L'Art du Brodeur* par Saint-Aubin). A later writer, while admitting the traditional skill of the Chinese embroiderers, points out that much of their work was in response to a commercial demand, and repetitive. 'La patience et l'habilité des artisans chinois, leur goût de la difficulté vaincue, leur amour du raffinement, même inutile, s'exercice à l'infini dans ce travail.' Their industry, he adds, was 'purement mercantile'. H. d'Ardenne de Tizac, *Les Etoffes de la Chine* (preface).

[3] Mrs Montagu in a letter to Sarah Robinson (1751) about some white satin flounces writes 'as you design them to be in white, they need only have the outline drawn on one flounce on the sleeves and robing'. *Elizabeth Montagu, Queen of the Blue Stockings*, ed. E. J. Clemenson, 1906, Vol. I, p. 280.

The symbolism of Chinese ornament was naturally not interpreted by French purchasers. La Fontaine describes sightseers at the palace of Versailles looking at the hangings, bed and chairs of Chinese needlework covered with figures illustrating the country's religion 'which they could not understand'.[1] In the design of the first painted Chinese silks brought to France fabulous monsters were represented which were unpopular, and were termed 'furies'. The floral designs, however, were universally acceptable, and designs of flowers and birds are frequently mentioned.[2] Evelyn[3] noted among a collection of rarities sent from the Jesuits of Japan and China to their order at Paris, and brought to London by ships of the East India Company 'glorious vests' embroidered with 'flowers, trees, beasts, birds, wrought in a kind of sleve silk very natural', and also the liveliness of the colours 'that for splendour and vividness we have nothing in Europe that approaches it'. The observation of nature and skilful stylization of the ornament were also acceptable.

Catholic missions, which were active in China, set up workshops for their support and dispatched to Europe vestments embroidered by them. An example of this work is a wall hanging of cream satin, embroidered in coloured silks in China for a Christian community, with St Anthony of Padua carrying the Infant Jesus. In the background cherub heads are framed in characteristic cloud forms (Fig. 141).

A great variety of stitches were used by the Chinese, satin stitch being the most common. In some embroideries, such as shawls both sides of the material are alike, and two workers were employed who sit on either side of a frame and push the needle through the material from one side to the other.

The method of enriching fabrics with gilt paper is indigenous to China and Japan.[4] Le Comte describes the Chinese embroidery in which silver or gold is used as 'wrought after a manner particular to them alone, for whereas in Europe we draw the gold as fine as possibly it can be twisted with the thread, the Chinese, to save the matter, or because they did not bethink themselves of this trick, satisfy themselves to gild or silver a long leaf of paper which they afterwards roll into little scrolls wherein they wrap the silk'.[5]

[1] *Les amours de Psyché* (1668). *Works* (ed. Raynal, viii, 31). 'C'est un tissu de la Chine plein de figures qui contiennent tout la religion de ce pays-là.'

[2] G. Townsend, 'Some notes on fashion in France in the seventeenth and eighteenth centuries', *Bulletin of the Museum of Fine Arts, Boston*. Vol. XLIV, No. 255.

[3] Evelyn, *Diary*, June 22nd, 1664.

[4] 'Leur industrie s'est toujours bornée a rouler leurs soies dans des papiers dorés, ou à appliquer les étoffes sur les papiers mêmes. Les deux méthodes sont également vicieuses.' G. T. Raynal, *Histoire philosophique et politique des établissements et du commerce des Européens dans les Indes*, 1770 (ed. 1780).

[5] Le Comte, *The Empire of China* (trs. 1737), pp. 138–9.

From the eighteenth century onwards painted silks and gauzes were exported, the designs being painted in body colours. Painted and embroidered gauze, stretched on a frame of wood, was used in China for the inner windows of a house, and Sir George Staunton describes such panels of silk gauze 'worked with the needle in flowers, fruit, birds and insects and others painted in watercolours'[1] (Fig. 137). Chinese pictures on gauze served as curtains in Mrs Montagu's Chinese dressing-room in Hill Street, which, according to contemporary account, 'resembled the temple of an Indian God'.[2]

Chinese silks painted in body colours with floral designs which closely followed European textile designs of the late eighteenth century, were in fashion for costumes (Fig. 138).

[1] Sir George Staunton, *Embassy*, Vol. II, p. 139.

[2] Mrs Montagu's famous Chinese dressing-room at Hill Street 'resembled the temple of an Indian God. The very curtains are Chinese pictures on gauze'. Jan. 3rd, 1750. *Letters & Journals of Lady Mary Coke.*

APPENDICES

A

MS Letter from Father de Mailla (from Jehol), dated October 26th, 1720, to Orry, Chinese Mission at Paris:

'Dans mes lettres de l'an passé [que je n'ai pas encore retrouvées], je vous marquay l'heureuse arrivée en Chine de nos chers frères Rousset et Gravereau; l'accueil favorable que l'empereur [K'anghi] leur fit en Tartarie, ou il les vit pour la première fois: l'espérance de Sa Majesté d'en profiter avantageusement et la joye que nous avions tous du service insigne que vous nous avies rendu en nous les envoyants [*sic*], non seulement à notre mission francoise, mais encore à toute notre mission de Chine. Permettés-moi, mon, Révérend Père, de vous dire le succès que l'un et l'autre ont eu dans leur employ depuis le temps qu'ils sont en Chine. . . . Si le frère Gravereau ne s'étoit appliqué en Europe qu'à l'émail, comme le frère Rousset à la chirurgie, sans doute qu'il auroit mieux réussi qu'il n'a fait. Mais deux choses luy ont un peu fait tort. La première qu'il a trouvé en arrivant icy, qu'on n'y estoit pas tout à fait ignorant sur l'émail. Et effectivement on peut dire que les Chinois, qui n'y travaillent que depuis cinq ou six ans par les ordres de Sa Majesté, y ont fait un progrès considérable. Le frère Gravereau est cependant encore leur maître et si ce cher frère, au lieu de s'occuper à plusieurs autres occupations qui n'ont servies [*sic*] qu'à le distraire de la principale, qui estoit l'émail, certaines pièces que les mandarins Chinois trouvent moyen de se procurer sur les vaisseaux venus d'Europe et qu'ils offrent à l'empereur ne lui nuiroient pas, et c'est la seconde chose, que l'ai dis [*sic*] qui luy a fait tort. Sa Majesté estime sa peinture, mais il le souhaitteroit plus habile en émail.' [Communicated by Father Henri Bernard—Maître.]

B

A contract was made with Sinqua on August 19th for chinaware 'to be delivered early for the Ships of next Season' (presumably for delivery in the autumn of 1773, since they could not be delivered in the autumn next following), in the quantities as follows:

		Tls.
350 Table Services, long dishes, blue and white (each 18 dishes, 8 to 18 in., 60 plates, 20 soup plates, 1 tureen to 2 sets)	each set	12.6.0.0
100 Table Services, round dishes, blue and white	,, ,,	10.0.0.0
300 sets Salad Dishes, 4 of sizes 9–12 in.	,, ,,	6.0.0
45 Bowls, size 2 gallons	each	1.0.0.0
45 Bowls, size 1½ gallons	,,	8.0.0
105 Bowls, size 4 quarts	,,	3.0.0
300 Bowls, size 3 quarts	,,	2.5.0
900 Bowls, size 2 quarts	,,	1.5.0
1,650 Bowls, size 3 pints	,,	1.2.0
2,550 Bowls, size 1 quart	,,	0.9.0

			Tls.
3,150 Bowls, size 1½ pints	.. ..	each	0.7.0
16,000 Basons, size 1 pint ..	.. ..	,,	0.4.8
20,000 Basons, size ½ pint ..	.. ..	,,	0.3.4
5,000 Breakfast Cups and Saucers	.. ..	pair	0.7.5
80,000 Single Plates, blue and white	.. ..	each	0.3.3
2,000 Soup Plates ..	.. ..	,,	0.4.3
5,000 Flat Water Plates ..	.. ..	,,	0.2.4
8,100 Deep Water Saucers	.. ..	,,	0.2.6
1,800 Sugar Dishes and Tops	.. ..	,,	0.7.0
7,500 Coffee Cans ..	.. ..	,,	0.1.4
1,050 Tea Pots ..	.. ..	,,	1.0.0
750 Milk Ewers ..	.. ..	,,	1.0.0
750 Sets of 3 Patty Pans	.. ..	set	1.5.0
360 Tea Services (43 pieces each)	.. ..	,,	1.0.0.0
39,000 Large Tea Cups and Saucers	.. ..	pair	0.4.2
87,000 Small Tea Cups and Saucers	.. ..	,,	0.2.6
2,400 sets of long Dishes, 10, 11, 12 in.	.. ..	set	5.5.0
600 sets of round Dishes, 10, 11, 12 in.	.. ..	,,	4.5.0

The sum involved under the contract was a total of Tls. 17,780 to provide the flooring for the east.
(*N.B.* £1 equalled three taels)

Extract from *The East India Company Trading to China*, by H. B. Morse, Vol. V.

C

In the sale of the Beckford Collection at Fonthill Abbey in September and October 1823 there were, if rightly described, ten lots of eggshell plates and basins:

	£	s.	d.
11*th day. Lot* 66			
Four fine Eggshell plates, red underneath with flowers and butterflies	1	8	0
Lot 87			
Sixteen plates of Eggshell China delicately pencilled in landscapes	3	13	6
12*th day. Lot* 126			
Six most delicate and fine Eggshell plates flowered and with rich borders	2	0	0
Lot 127			
Three ditto (lady and children) red underneath	1	6	0
13*th day. Lot* 253			
Three Eggshell basons and covers with butterflies and flowers		19	0
Lot 262			
Five of the finest Eggshell plates, variously figured, pink underneath	2	15	0
Lot 263			
Six ditto representing Chinese fishermen with flowers on the outside	2	8	0
15*th day. Lot* 505			
Nine delicate and beautiful eggshell plates with double border and flowers	5	15	6
18*th day. Lot* 906			
Six fine eggshell plates, pink ground with double Mosaic and flowered border with various conversational subjects painted in a superior manner	6	6	0
Lot 907			
Five ditto, 3 and 2	5	5	0

D

Records of the Importation of Lacquer

1690

'Your lacquered ware its so slight and nought, and of such low esteem here that it will not defray ye charges of ye freights.' [Letter from the East India Company to their chief and Council at Tonking, May 24th, 1690: MS Records of the East India Company.]

1691

'Hopes that better and cheaper goods will be provided than those you sent home last by Capt Pool, wch turn'd to a very discouraging acct & your lacquered ware especeally is of little or no value, not worth the freight being abundantly outdone by what we receive from China.' [Letter, dated February 18th, 1691, from the same to the same.]

1697

List of goods proper to be invested in the ship *Trumball*, at Amoy, October 26th, 1697. 'If any fine lacquer or Right Japan cabenetts or skreens to be had you may bring some. All sorts of useful things in fine Japan lacquer but bring little or no ordinary lacquer ware.' [East India Company's Instructions. MS Records of the East India Company.]

1697

'What tonnage will yet remain to be completed you may partly supply, with some more boards of sufficient thickness (three-quarters of an inch or thereabouts) lacquered on both sides, fit for screens, or pannels to be done by the best artists, and of the finest Lacker & works procurable, or else none at all.' [Company's instructions for the supra cargoes of the ship *Trumball* galley, bound for Amoy in China [October 27th, 1697]. MS Records of the East India Company.]

[1699, but undated]

[Directions about lacquered ware.] The China factory is asked to provide:

No. 1. Of this shape, 60 cabinets, viz. 20 of the black ground, inlayed with mother-of-pearl with figures, 10 black & gold, 10 red & gold, 20 of engraved work, the ground gold, with Landscapes and figures. 20 sets of screens, 12 leaves of a set, 8, 9 & 10 feet high by 20 to 24 inches broad; black & gold, with Landscapes & figures engraved on a gold ground.

No. 2. Of this Desk fashion, 40 Tables of the same sorts as the cabinets.

No. 3. Of this fashion 80 folding card tables, without Pillars, lacquered as the cabinets.

No. 4. Of this size, 500 tables, 200 black & gold, 200 red & gold, drawn with Birds; & 100 black, inlayed with mother of pearl with Figures.

No. 5. Of this size, 500 tables, in other respects as No. 4.

No. 6. Of this sort, 400, viz. 100 red & gold, 100 Black & gold, 50 plain Black, & 150 inlayed with mother of Pearl.

No. 7. Of this size 600, viz. 400 black & gold; 50 inlayed with mother of pearl; 100 red & gold; & 50, the ground black, painted with colours, but not engraved.

No. 8. Of this sort, 800.

Bring no skreens with silk sashes, but all to be of entire Japan work from top to bottom.

[*East India Company's Letter Book* (1697), p. 169]

THE
ILLUSTRATIONS

1. VIEW TAKEN FROM DANES ISLAND looking towards Canton at Whampoa, showing
East Indiamen at anchor. One ship flies the flag of the East India Company. Aquatint in colours.
Published by W. J. Huggins, 1835; printed by E. Duncan. $14\frac{3}{4} \times 23\frac{1}{2}$ in.

2. 'NEW CHINA STREET AT CANTON.' Coloured lithograph by Bichebois after a drawing
by Lauvergne, c. 1835. $11\frac{5}{8} \times 7\frac{3}{4}$ in.

3. 'CANTON.' An engraving by G. Child, *c.* 1750. $11\frac{3}{8} \times 7\frac{1}{8}$ in.

4. 'THE EUROPEAN FACTORIES AT CANTON.' Lithograph by Cicéri after a drawing by Borget, *c.* 1840. $16 \times 9\frac{7}{8}$ in.

5. 'MACAO BAY.' Drawing by Duché de Vancy. Engraved by Masquelier *c.* 1797. 15¾ × 10 in.

6. MACAO BAY (1834). Drawing from a sketch-book of George Chinnery (*c.* 1766–1846). Ink on paper. 10½ × 7 in. *The British Museum.*

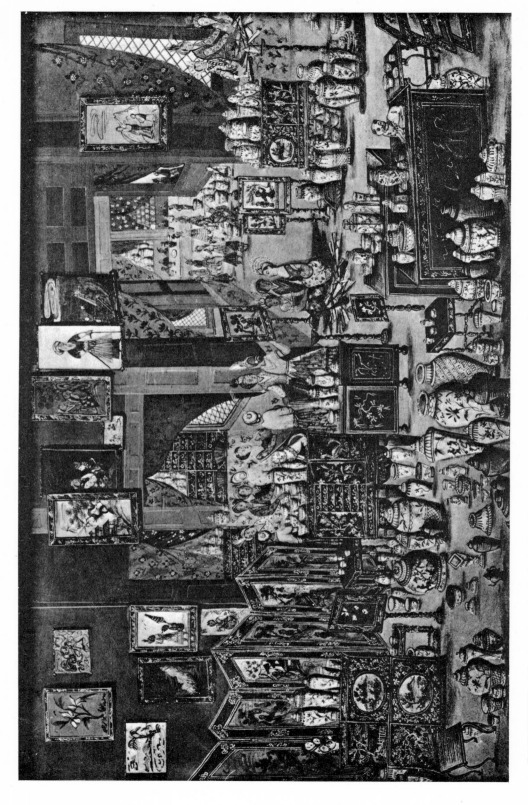

7. PAINTING of the interior of a dealer's shop (probably either in an Indo-China port or on the Coromandel Coast) showing Chinese export porcelain, pictures, and lacquered furniture. 10⅝ ×17 ⅞ in. *The Victoria and Albert Museum.*

8. A CHINESE PAINTING IN OIL for the export market. From a volume of sketches of Chinese trades made for the European market. Body colour on paper. $11\frac{7}{10} \times 14\frac{1}{2}$ in. *The British Museum*.

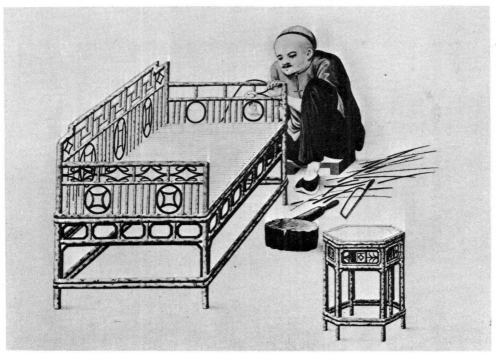

9. A CHINESE MAKING RATTAN FURNITURE for the export market. From a volume of sketches of Chinese trades. $11\frac{7}{10} \times 14\frac{1}{2}$ in. *The British Museum*.

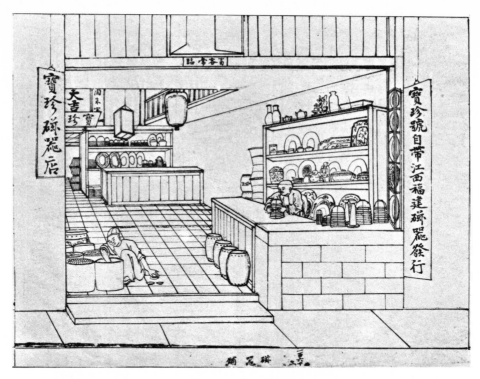

10. PORCELAIN STORE. From a volume of ink sketches of trades made for the European market. 18 × 13 in. *The British Museum.*

11. COMMERCIAL PAINTERS IN STUDIO AND SHOP. From a volume of ink sketches of Chinese trades made for the European market. 18 × 13 in. *The British Museum.*

12. LEAF OF A SCREEN depicting hunting scenes, in
carved and coloured lacquer. Chinese; seventeenth century.
The Victoria and Albert Museum.

13. SIXFOLD LACQUER SCREEN. K'ang Hsi period (1660–1722). 7 ft. 4 in. × 10 ft.
Mr Simon Yorke, Erthig Park, Denbighshire.

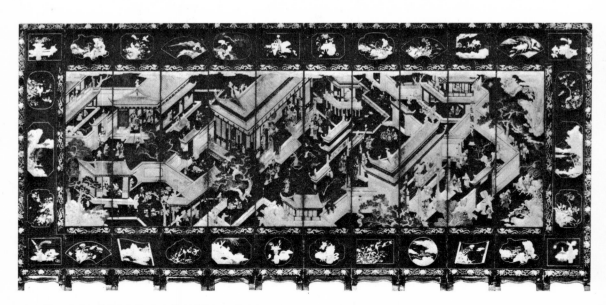

14. TWELVEFOLD LACQUER SCREEN. Dated 1690. *The Metropolitan Museum, New York.*

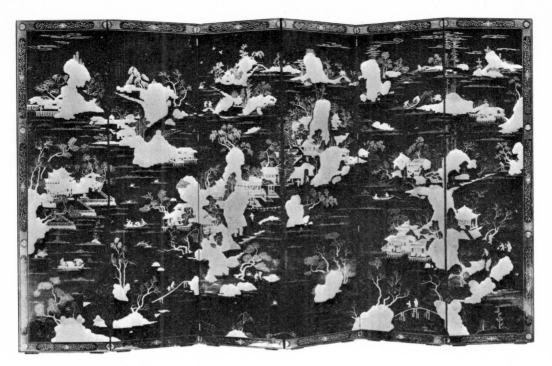

15. SIXFOLD SCREEN lacquered in gold on a black ground. First half of the eighteenth century. Height 7 ft. 2 in.; width 12 ft. *The Victoria and Albert Museum.*

16. TWELVEFOLD LACQUER SCREEN. K'ang Hsi period (1660-1722). *Messrs M. Harris and Sons.*

17. FOURFOLD LACQUER SCREEN. Early eighteenth century. Height 5 ft. 8 in. *S. D. Winkworth Collection*.

18. LACQUERED SCREEN OF SIX PANELS. Dated 1781. Height 7 ft:, approx. *Mrs Lilian Duff*.

19. CHEST overlaid with incised lacquer; the carved and gilt stand of the late seventeenth century. *The Marquess of Northampton, Castle Ashby.*

20. CABINET of incised and painted lacquer. Early eighteenth century. Height (not including stand), 2 ft. 6 in. approx., width (doors shut), 3 ft. approx. *Mr J. Sykes.*

22. MIRROR, the frame overlaid with sections of incised lacquer. Height 6 ft. ¾ in.; width 3 ft. 3 in. *The Duke of Buccleuch, Boughton House, Northamptonshire.*

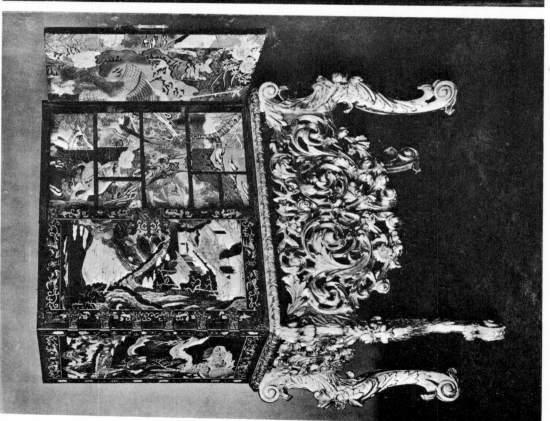

21. CABINET overlaid with sections of incised lacquer from a screen. The carved and gilt stand dates from the late seventeenth century. *The Marquess of Northampton, Castle Ashby.*

23. BUREAU CABINET (one of a pair) lacquered in gold on a black ground. Late eighteenth century. *Mereworth Castle, Kent*.

24. BUREAU CABINET lacquered in gold on a black ground. Feet carved and gilt. Eighteenth century. *The Victoria and Albert Museum*.

25. CHEST overlaid with panels of incised lacquer, the lacquer taken from a
room at Chatsworth which was still in position in 1724. The stand dates from
about that period. 3 ft. 8 in ×5 ft. 4½ in. *The Duke of Devonshire, Chatsworth.*

26. CHEST overlaid with panels of incised lacquer. Early eighteenth century.
3 ft. 2½ in ×4 ft. 9½ in. *The Earl of Verulam, Gorhambury, Herts.*

27. COMMODE overlaid with panels of incised Chinese lacquer, probably from a screen. *c.* 1760. 2 ft. 8¾ in. × 3 ft. 10¼ in. *The Marquess of Bristol, Ickworth, Suffolk.*

28. DRESSING TABLE, framing Chinese lacquer panels on sides, combined with English japanning on front. Height, with mirror, 4 ft. 5 in. *The Phillip Sassoon Collection.*

29. TABLE TOP of lacquer inlaid with mother-of-pearl. *c.* 1720. 1 ft. 8½ in. ×2 ft. 10½ in. *The Duchess of Roxburghe Collection.*

30. PLATEAU OR TABLE CENTRE of wood lacquered in red and gold on a black ground. Made for the European market about 1800. Length 6 ft. 1¼ in., width 1 ft. 11½ in. *The Victoria and Albert Museum.*

31. JAPANESE LAC-
QUER CABINET on.
English gilt stand.
Seventeenth century.
(*Whereabouts unknown.*)

32. JAPANESE BOX
lacquered in gold on a
black ground. Late
eighteenth century.
(This box belonged to
Lord Macartney,
British Ambassador to
China 1792-94.) *Wynd-
ham Clark Esq*, 44
Berkeley Square, London.

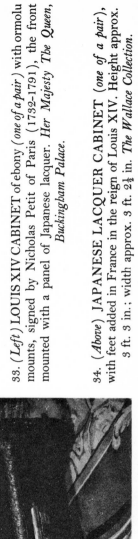

33. (*Left*) LOUIS XIV CABINET of ebony (*one of a pair*) with ormolu mounts, signed by Nicholas Petit of Paris (1732-1791), the front mounted with a panel of Japanese lacquer. *Her Majesty The Queen, Buckingham Palace.*

34. (*Above*) JAPANESE LACQUER CABINET (*one of a pair*), with feet added in France in the reign of Louis XIV. Height approx. 3 ft. 3 in.; width approx. 3 ft. 2½ in. *The Wallace Collection.*

35. BEDROOM, the walls decorated with Chinese wall paper painted with a design of flowering shrubs, hung by Thomas Chippendale in 1769. *Lord St Oswald, Nostell Priory, Yorkshire.*

36. PANEL OF WALL PAPER (one of a set of four) painted with flowering shrubs and peacocks. Eighteenth century. Height 8 ft.; width 4 ft. *The Victoria and Albert Museum.*

37. PANEL OF WALL PAPER (one of a set of three). Late eighteenth century. 11 ft. 3 in. × 3 ft. 10½ in. *The Victoria and Albert Museum.*

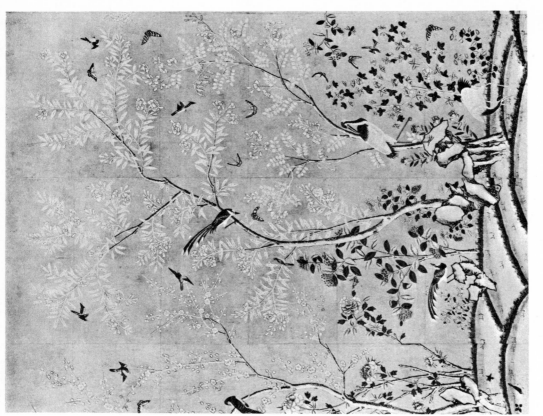

38. PANEL OF WALL PAPER representing huntsmen chasing deer. Eighteenth century. *Mr Tufnell Joliffe, Lockleys, Hertfordshire.*

39. PANEL OF WALL PAPER painted with flowering shrubs and birds. *c.* 1800. *Mrs Townley-Balfour, Townley Hall, Ireland.*

40. TWO PANELS FROM A WALL PAPER, adjacent panels from a continuous scene, partly printed from wood blocks and partly painted in tempera. Middle of the eighteenth century. Height 7 ft. 11 in.; width 2 ft. 11 in. *The Victoria and Albert Museum.*

41. PORTION OF A WALL PAPER from The Old Brewery House, Watford. Early eighteenth century. 4 ft. 5 in. × 2 ft. 10¾ in. *The Victoria and Albert Museum.*

42. DETAIL OF A WALL PAPER painted with scenes from Chinese life. Late eighteenth century. *Sir Francis Burdett, Bt, Ramsbury, Wilts.*

43. WALL PAPER representing a mountainous landscape. Height 6 ft. 4 in. *Viscount Allendale, Bretton Park, Yorkshire.*

44 & 45. DETAILS OF A WALL PAPER, illustrating scenes from Chinese life. *Mr Ernest Thesiger*.

46. ROOM hung after 1815 with Chinese paintings in gilt paper frames. *Clifton Hall, Northamptonshire.*

47. FLOWER GARDENS AT CHIH-TOW, CANTON, from a volume of sketches of the temples, buildings, and gardens of Canton, made for the foreign market. Water colour on paper. 20 × 15 in. *The British Museum.*

48. MANDARIN RIDING IN HIS CHAIR. From a book of sketches of Chinese ceremonies and processions, made for the foreign market. Water colour on paper. $18\frac{1}{3} \times 14\frac{1}{5}$ in. *The British Museum.*

49. A CHINESE LANDSCAPE from a volume containing fifty original views of the interior of China, 'executed by the best artists of China' for export. *c.* 1795. $17\frac{1}{2} \times 12\frac{1}{2}$ in. E Lansdowne collection. (*Lord Lansdowne died in 1805 and his collection was purchased by The British Museum in* 1807.)

50. **PAINTING IN BODY COLOUR ON LINEN** of an Imperial audience given by the Emperor Chia Ching (1791-1820) brought back to England about 1800 by Richard Hill, sometime supercargo of the East India Company. 2 ft. 7 in. × 3 ft. 2 in. *The Royal Pavilion, Brighton.*

51. 'RICE PAPER' DRAWING of a butterfly, mallow flowers, and insects, made for export. Early nineteenth century. $10 \times 6\frac{5}{8}$ in.

52. (*Right*) COLOURED WOODCUT of woman and child. $9\frac{1}{2} \times 16$ in. *The British Museum.*

54. MIRROR, painted with a river landscape and birds. The English frame is carved and gilded and dates from about 1750. *Messrs Botibol.*

53. MIRROR, the lower panel painted with Chinese buildings and figures; the frame in rococo taste. Middle of the eighteenth century. *Owner unknown.*

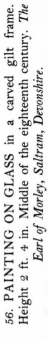

56. PAINTING ON GLASS in a carved gilt frame. Height 2 ft. 4 in. Middle of the eighteenth century. *The Earl of Morley, Saltram, Devonshire.*

55. PAINTING ON GLASS in a carved gilt frame. Height 3 ft. 7 in. Middle of the eighteenth century. *The Earl of Morley, Saltram, Devonshire.*

57. PAINTING ON GLASS of a female figure in a pastoral landscape. *c.* 1760. *Messrs Botibol.*

58. PAINTING ON GLASS of a female figure in a pastoral landscape (the same subject as in Fig. 57, but reversed). The pierced and carved frame, *c.* 1760.

59. PAINTING ON GLASS of a figure
in European dress in an English carved and
gilt frame. *c.* 1760. (*Whereabouts unknown.*)

60. PAINTING ON GLASS of a group in a river
landscape. The Chinese frame lacquered and gilt.
H.M. Queen Mary.

61. MIRROR, painted with a group of Chinese in a river landscape. In an English pierced and carved frame, *c.* 1750. *Messrs Blairman.*

62. MIRROR, painted with group of Chinese in a pavilion. The Chinese frame lacquered. *Messrs Blairman.*

63. BUREAU CABINET in padouk, the two cupboard doors
mounted with Chinese pictures on mirror glass. Middle of the
eighteenth century. *Messrs Blairman*.

64. TWO MIRROR PANELS painted with Chinese figures in a pavilion. The gilt frame attributed to Thomas Chippendale, *c.* 1765. *The Earl of Harewood, Harewood House.*

65. MIRROR, painted after an engraving of Radnor House, Twickenham. Late eighteenth century

66. PAINTING ON GLASS of the Emperor Chia Ching (1796–1820) giving an audience in winter, probably at Jehol. Brought back about 1800 by Amyand John Hall, supercargo of the East India Company. 3 ft. 9½ in. ×6 ft. 3 in. *The Victoria and Albert Museum.*

67. PAINTING IN OIL AND WATER-COLOUR ON GLASS of a female figure in European dress wearing a veil, after an unidentified engraving. Signed 'Falqua Pinxit'. *Mr Basil and the Hon. Mrs Ionides, Buxted Park, Sussex.*

68. PAINTING ON GLASS after a European engraving of Venus and Cupid; the original engraved by R. A. Meadows after the drawing by R. Westall, R.A., made in 1794. *Mr Basil and the Hon. Mrs Ionides, Buxted Park, Sussex.*

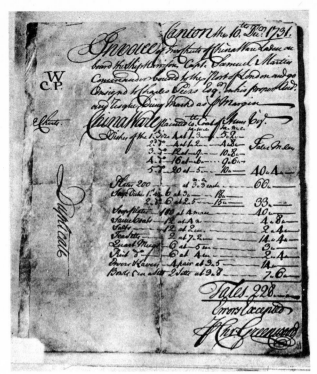

70. THE PEERS FAMILY'S BILL OF LADING FOR CHINAWARE, dated Canton, Dec. 10th 1731. *The British Museum.*

69. (*Above*) PLATE WITH ARMS OF THE PEERS FAMILY in enamels. Diam. 9½ in.
(*Below*) PLATE WITH CREST OF THE PEERS FAMILY in underglaze blue. Diam. 8⅞ in. *The British Museum.*

71. (*Right*) CUP, decorated in China with the Royal Coat of Arms and the date 1747. Height 2½ in. *The British Museum.*

72. STANDING FIGURE OF A MANDARIN WITH NODDING HEAD, enamelled in black and colours. Eighteenth century. Height 15½ in. *Mr Basil and the Hon. Mrs Ionides, Buxted Park, Sussex.*

73. VESSEL formed of a figure of a European seated on a mound (which is fitted with a tap). Enamelled in colours. Eighteenth century. *Mr Basil and the Hon. Mrs Ionides, Buxted Park, Sussex.*

74. FIGURE OF A GIRL IN DUTCH DRESS,
wearing a ruff and apron. Enamelled in colours. One
of a pair. Eighteenth century. Height 17½ in. *Mr
Basil and the Hon. Mrs Ionides, Buxted Park, Sussex.*

75. FIGURE OF A EUROPEAN GIRL
wearing a short-sleeved coat over an under-
dress, and a cap. Enamelled in colours. One
of a pair. Eighteenth century. Height 17½
in. *Mr Basil and the Hon. Mrs Ionides,
Buxted Park, Sussex*

76. PLATE, with the arms of Okeover impaling Nicholl, 1743. Diam. 8⅞ in. *The British Museum.*

77. PLATE, decorated with the arms of Compton. *c.* 1730. Diam. 18½ in. *The Marquess of Northampton, Castle Ashby, Northamptonshire.*

78. PLATE, decorated with the arms of Catherine the Great of Russia. Late eighteenth century. Diam. 9¼ in. *Mr Basil and the Hon. Mrs Ionides, Buxted Park, Sussex.*

79. PLATE, decorated with the arms of Lee of Caton in Warwickshire: on the rim, panels of views of the port of London and the harbour of Canton. Made for Eldred Lancelot Lee before 1734. Diam. 9⅞ in. *Mr Basil and the Hon. Mrs Ionides, Buxted Park, Sussex.*

80. COFFEE POT AND COVER, decorated with the arms of Clifford. Yung Chêng period (1722-35). Height, with cover, 10 in. *The British Museum*.

81. COFFEE POT AND TWO COVERED CUPS AND SAUCERS, decorated in underglaze blue with European figures and scenes. The cups inscribed round the lips 'L'Empire de la vertu est établi jusqu'au bout de l'univers'. K'ang Hsi (1660-1722). *Mr Basil and the Hon. Mrs Ionides, Buxted Park, Sussex*.

114

82. VASE decorated in monochrome on one side with a portrait of Martin Luther (the pair to this vase is decorated with a portrait of Calvin). Eighteenth century. Height 8⅝ in. *Mr Basil and the Hon. Mrs Ionides, Buxted Park, Sussex.*

83. PUNCH BOWL decorated in monochrome on one side with a boor smoking and another drinking. Eighteenth century. Diam. 11⅝ in. *Mr Basil and the Hon. Mrs Ionides, Buxted Park, Sussex.*

84. PLATE, decorated in gold and monochrome with a group in European costume. Eighteenth century. Diam. 9 in. *The British Museum.*

85. PLATE, decorated in monochrome with the Resurrection of Christ. Eighteenth century. Diam. $8\frac{7}{8}$ in. *The British Museum.*

86. BOWL, decorated in underglaze blue with the Crucifixion. Early eighteenth century. Diam. $5\frac{7}{8}$ in. *The British Museum.*

87. PLATE, decorated in monochrome with the
Baptism of Christ. Eighteenth century. Diam. 9 in.
The British Museum.

88. DISH, with a design after an engraving of
'The Triumph of Mordecai'. Eighteenth century.
16¾ in. *The British Museum.*

89. DISH, with a design in monochrome after an engraving of
the dipping of Achilles in the Styx. First half of the eighteenth
century. Diam. 16¼ in. *The British Museum.*

90. PLATE enamelled in colours with a nude girl lying on a couch. First half of the eighteenth century. Diam. 8 in. *Mr Basil and the Hon. Mrs Ionides, Buxted Park, Sussex.*

91. PLATE enamelled in colours with a representation of Joseph and Potiphar's wife, probably based on an engraving by Marcantonio Raimondi after Raphael. First half of the eighteenth century. *Mr Basil and the Hon. Mrs Ionides, Buxted Park, Sussex.*

92. PLATE, painted in black, red, and gilt in China, after a painting by Nicholas Lancret, *Les Oies du frère Philippe*. c. 1740. *The Victoria and Albert Museum.*

93. CUP AND SAUCER, decorated in underglaze blue with a siren rising from the waves, and inscribed *Gardez vous de la syrene*. Diam. of saucer, 5½ in. Height of cup, 2 in. K'ang Hsi period (1662–1722). *The British Museum.*

94. PUNCH BOWL enamelled in colours with a rider on a packhorse. A milestone bears the inscription '4 miles from Horsham'. Second half of the eighteenth century. Diam. 17½ in. *Mr Basil and the Hon. Mrs Ionides, Buxted Park, Sussex.*

95. PUNCH BOWL enamelled with the Boscobel oak and with a small house, and a group of countrymen with pitchforks hunting for Charles II. Second half of the eighteenth century. Diam. 16¼ in. *Mr Basil and the Hon. Mrs Ionides, Buxted Park, Sussex.*

96. PUNCH BOWL, decorated on the side with a European cottage and men playing bowls. Second half of the eighteenth century. Diam. 11¾ in. *Mr Basil and the Hon. Mrs Ionides, Buxted Park, Sussex.*

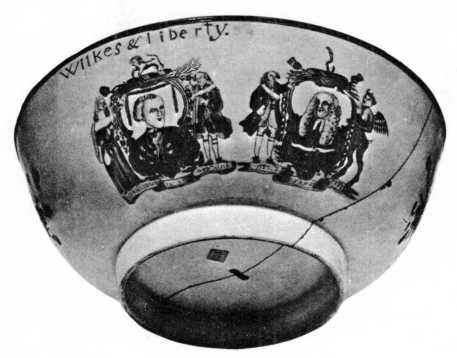

97. BOWL inscribed 'WILKES AND LIBERTY' and decorated with busts of John Wilkes and Lord Mansfield, Lord Chief Justice. *c.* 1763. Diam. 10⅞ in.
The British Museum.

98. CHINESE DISH painted in Europe with Dutch ship and the arms of Zealand and the date 1700. Diam. 8½ in. *The British Museum*.

99. DISH made and painted in China with a Dutch ship and the inscription CHRIST: SCHOONE-MAN OPPR: STUERMAN OP T'SCHIP VRYBURG: T FR: REEDE WANPHO IN CHINA INT. IAAR 1736.

100. CHINESE SAUCER DISH, painted in coloured enamels in Holland in Kakiemon style. Mark of the Dresden collection, N-63. (This collection was brought together by Augustus the Strong, King of Poland and Elector of Saxony, between about 1694 and 1715.) Diam. 9 in. *The British Museum.*

101. TWO-HANDED VASE, made and decorated in China. On the sides are classical tripods in red and gold. One of a pair. Late eighteenth century. Height 12½ in. *Mr Basil and the Hon. Mrs Ionides, Buxted Park, Sussex.*

102. (*Left*) TRAY of Chinese porcelain decorated with figures in colour and gilding in Europe, possibly in Venice. Diam. 5 in. *The British Museum.*
(*Right*) VASE AND COVER of Chinese porcelain decorated in Europe with figures, possibly in Venice. Height, with cover, 5 in.

103. (*Left*) TEA CADDY of European silver shape decorated in *famille verte* enamels on a blue ground. K'ang Hsi (1662–1722). Height (with lid), 4 in.
(*Centre*) SALT CELLAR decorated in *famille verte* enamels, K'ang Hsi period. Diam. at base $3\frac{1}{4}$ in.
(*Right*) JUG made at Tehua in Fukien. German stoneware shape. Early eighteenth century. Height $3\frac{3}{4}$ in. *All three in The British Museum.* (Franks Collection).

104. SAUCER DISH of Chinese porcelain painted in enamels in Europe, with horseman; inscribed on the back 'George II'. (In commemoration of the battle of Dettingen 1743.) Diam. 8½ in. *The British Museum*.

105. (*Left*) MUG, made and painted in China in celebration of the victory of Culloden, with bust of the Duke of Cumberland, and the date 1746. Height, 4 in.
(*Centre*) MUG, with masonic emblems and initials E. M., made and painted in China. Mid-eighteenth century. Height, 6¼ in.
(*Right*) MUG, made and painted in China with the bust of the Young Pretender, Prince Charles Edward. *c*. 1745. Height 4 in. *All three in the British Museum*.

106. (*Left*) VASE decorated in China in underglaze blue, with two coloured panels and touches of gilt added in Europe. Eighteenth century. Height 7¾ in.
(*Centre*) CHINESE BOTTLE decorated in China in underglaze red with monsters, and clobbered in Europe with figures and flowers in enamels. Height 8½ in.
(*Right*) CHINESE JAR painted in Europe with black and gold Chinoiserie, perhaps by Preissler. Height 9 in. *All three from the British Museum.*

107. (*Left*) CUP AND SAUCER of Chinese porcelain decorated in Europe with red and gilding by Preissler. Diam. of saucer 5½ in. *The British Museum.*
(*Right*) CHINESE PORCELAIN CUP, decorated in red in Europe with the miracle of the loaves and fishes. Signed CARLO WENDELIN ADVEITER DI ZIERNFEDE: FIERENZE. Height 3 in. *The British Museum.*

108. SIDE VIEW AND BOTTOM OF AN INCENSE BURNER, enamelled with pink and blue lotus on a yellow ground. From the Summer Palace, Peking. Mark and period of K'ang Hsi (1660–1722). Diam. approx. 2½ in. *John Morrison collection, Fonthill.*

109. (*Left*) BOWL enamelled with *millefleur* decoration on a green ground. Mark and period of K'ang Hsi (1660–1772). Diam. 6½ in. *The British Museum.*
(*Right*) BOWL enamelled with sprays of plum blossom on a ruby ground. Mark and period of K'ang Hsi. Diam. 6 in. *The British Museum.*

110. DISH, enamelled with white birds and pink and yellow flowers in the Chinese taste. Yung Chêng period (1723–1735). Diam. 8½ in. *Messrs Spink.*

111. PAIR OF WINE CUPS, decorated in coloured enamels on a white ground. Mark and period of Ch'ien Lung (1736–1795). Height 1¼ in. *The British Museum.*
VASE, decorated with quails and flowers in colours on a yellow enamel ground. Mark and period of Ch'ien Lung. Height 5 in. *The British Museum.*

112. GOURD-SHAPED VASE, enamelled with a design of gourds and tendrils on a yellow ground, with panels of butterflies and flowers on a white ground. Ch'ien Lung period (1736-1795). Height approx. 6½ in. *Mr and Mrs Alfred Clark.*

113. VASE enamelled with churches in a landscape under white clouds in a blue sky. Peking work (possibly by a European). Mark and period of Ch'ien Lung (1736-1795). Height 9 in. *Mr R. S. Jenyns.*

114. KETTLE ON A SPIRIT LAMP
enamelled in *famille rose* colours. Ch'ien
Lung period. *Mrs Berridge.*

115. WINE EWER enamelled with
rosettes in colour on a white ground.
Ch'ien Lung period. *Messrs Spink.*

116. WINE EWER with figures in European style; probably Peking work. Tao
Kuang or later. *Mr R. S. Jenyns.*

117. WINE EWER enamelled in *famille
rose* colours. Ch'ien Lung period. *Mr and
Mrs Alfred Clark.*

118. DISH enamelled in colours with design of dragon among clouds. Ch'ien Lung period (1736-1795). Diam. 10½ in. *The British Museum.*

119. VASE enamelled with figures in a landscape surrounded by floral motives on a yellow ground. Probably Peking work. Eighteenth century. Height 16¾ in. *Messrs Spink.*

120. INCENSE-BURNER, of gilt bronze with enamel decoration. Of eighteenth-century workmanship. Height 3½ in. approx. *From the S. D. Winkworth collection.*

121. COVERED CUP with European metal mount enamelled with European figures. Peking work. Yung Chêng period (1723-1735). Height 5½ in. *The British Museum.*

122. PLAQUE overlaid with enamel and painted with a European woman reading to children in a landscape scene. Eighteenth century. 6⅛ × 4¾ in. *Mr Basil and the Hon. Mrs Ionides, Buxted Park, Sussex*

123. TEABOWL AND COVER. Enamelled on the outside with peonies in colour on a white ground; inside lavender blue. Probably Peking work. Ch'ien Lung period (1736-1795). Height 4½ in. approx. *Mr and Mrs Alfred Clark.*

124. IVORY CASKET, carved in relief and painted with a design of figures on the lid and flowers on the sides; silver feet. Inside, two silver tea caddies bearing the London hallmark 1742. Length $9\frac{1}{2}$ in.; width $5\frac{5}{8}$ in. *Mr Basil and the Hon. Mrs Ionides, Buxted Park, Sussex.*

125. CASKET of pierced and carved ivory, containing two cut-glass tea caddies. Eighteenth century. Height $4\frac{1}{2}$ in.; width $10\frac{1}{8}$ in. *Mr Basil and the Hon. Mrs Ionides, Buxted Park, Sussex.*

126. CASKET decorated with engraved, pierced, and carved plaques of mother-of-pearl and mounted with Chinese medallions of painted glass. Eighteenth century. Height 5 in.; length 10½ in. *Mr Basil and the Hon. Mrs Ionides, Buxted Park, Sussex.*

127. CASKET mounted with plaques of mother-of-pearl, carved in low relief. Eighteenth century. Height 6 in.; length 7 in. *Mr Basil and the Hon. Mrs Ionides, Buxted Park, Sussex.*

128. (*Top left*) AN IVORY GROUP (*Top right*) SOAPSTONE FIGURE. Both from the Sloane collection (acquired in 1753). Height $3\frac{2}{5}$ in. and $3\frac{1}{5}$ in. respectively. *The British Museum.*

129. (*Left*) STANDING FIGURE IN CLASSI-CAL DRESS, WITH DOG, in carved soapstone. Eighteenth century. Height $6\frac{1}{2}$ in. *Mr Basil and the Hon. Mrs Ionides, Buxted Park, Sussex.*

130. (*Bottom*) RHINOCEROS-HORN LIBA-TION CUPS. Height $3\frac{1}{8}$ and 3 in. respectively. *From the Sloane Collection.*

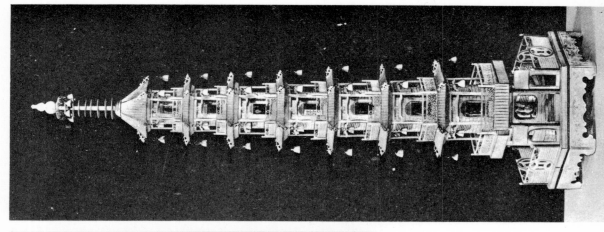

131. CARVED IVORY FAN made for the European market. Late eighteenth century.
Width 9⅞ in. *Mr R. S. Jenyns.*

132. PAGODA of mother-of-pearl with perforated galleries. Late eighteenth or early nineteenth century. *Mr Basil and the Hon. Mrs Ionides, Buxted Park, Sussex.*

136

133. TORTOISE-SHELL BOX carved in high relief. Cantonese work of the early nineteenth century. Diam. 3½ in. *W. W. Winkworth Esq.* (Photograph by Victor Furst).

134. CARVED BOXWOOD FRAME with scenes from Chinese life, made for the European market. Early nineteenth century. Outside 10×9 in.; inside 6×4 in.
Mr L. G. Creed.

135. SILK CHASUBLE painted with flowers. Eighteenth century. Size, 3 ft. 6 in. ×2 ft. 4 in.
The Victoria and Albert Museum.

136. LADY'S SILK DRESS painted in China. *c.* 1760. Length, 5 ft. *The Victoria and Albert Museum.*

137. GAUZE HANGING with panels of birds, flowers and insects, painted and woven in China for the European market. Eighteenth century. *Mr Basil and the Hon. Mrs Ionides, Buxted Park, Sussex.*

138. FRAGMENT OF AN OYSTER WHITE CHINESE SATIN HANGING painted with flowers for the European market. Eighteenth century. 3 ft 6 in. × 2 ft. 4 in. *Lord de Saumarez, Shrubland Park, Ipswich, Suffolk.*

139. ALTAR FRONTAL embroidered with the arms of Don Fernando Valdis Tamon, Knight of Santiago, Governor and Captain General of the Phillipines. *c.* 1737. Probably made for the Governor's Chapel by Chinese in Manila. Size 3 ft. 5 in. × 6 ft. 9 in. *The Victoria and Albert Museum*

140. SILK PANEL with a design of flowers in body colours in European taste, painted in China for the European market. Eighteenth century. *Mr Basil and the Hon. Mrs Ionides, Buxted Park, Sussex.*

141. HANGING OF EMBROIDERED SATIN, depicting St Anthony of Padua and the Infant Saviour; worked by Chinese craftsmen for a Christian community. Early eighteenth century. Length 5 ft. 8¾ in.; width 4 ft. 4¾ in. *The Victoria and Albert Museum.*

142. **CHINESE EMBROIDERY** in coloured silks on a yellow ground, carrying the arms of the first Duke of Chandos within a framework of blue European velvet. (The arms impaled are those of his second wife, thus dating the work between the years 1719 and 1735.) *The Victoria and Albert Museum.*

143. BED COVER of red silk, embroidered in coloured floss silks and gold threads. Seventeenth century. 10 × 9 ft. approx. *The Marquis of Salisbury, Hatfield, Hertfordshire.*

144. PORTION OF A SHAWL of buff-coloured silk, embroidered in colours. Late eighteenth century, or first half of the nineteenth century. *The Victoria and Albert Museum.*

INDEX

INDEX